CW01308166

Design & Meditation

Improving health, healthcare and quality of life

Vitality N. 2

Design & Meditation
Improving health, healthcare and quality of life
by Alessandro Caruso

Copyright © 2024 Alessandro Caruso
First Edition

Publisher: The Ran Network
info@therannetwork.com
https://therannetwork.com

Cover art: Massimo Assenza
Layout design: Simone Chierchini

No part of this book can be reproduced or used in any form or by any means without prior written permission of the publisher

ISBN: 9798325627750

Imprint: Independently published on Amazon KDP

Alessandro Caruso

Design & Meditation

Improving health, healthcare and quality of life

The Ran Network

To my Mum, for the unshakeable confidence you've always had in me, long before knowing what my path in life would be. Despite living away from home most of my life with long periods of silence, your faith in me has fuelled my motivation at every major crossroads, to transform my ordinary life with extra-ordinary deeds.

Table of Contents

Preface by Dr W Ruga — 10

Introduction — 14

Background — 16

Existential context — 23

   Life journey — 24

     Born — 25

     A family business — 32

     University — 40

     Accident — 44

     Amelia — 53

     A stranger in a foreign land — 62

Festina Lente	74
Change	78
Clearing and awareness	80
Enthusiasm of a child	82
"One day without work is a day without eating."	86
Who is our design for?	92
Why am I doing this?	96
A nurturing environment	98
Interdependent	101
The next step	104
Studio	110
A harmonious language	122
Empathic curiosity	130
Creative wellbeing	152
Foreground	174
Afterword by Amelia Caruso	178
Acknowledgements	185
Recommended readings	184
About the author	188
Photo credits	191

Preface

Who, what, why, where, when, and how – these are the key elements of every good story. Indeed, each one of these elements is addressed in what may initially appear to be a fairly conventional autobiography about an architect called Alessandro Caruso and his projects. However – there is nothing conventional about Alex's story.

Uniquely, this is an account of a reflexive journey that dives deeply into the explication of the 'how': how is it that Alex's father is an architect and architecture is the family business that Alex was born into, how is it that certain life events have critically shaped Alex's life journey to prepare him for discovering and becoming his purpose, how is it that Alex actually does create buildings that really do improve health, healthcare, and quality of life?

Is it a coincidence that certain life events shape our lives? There is a Zen koan that touches upon this question, it asks us to: *'Show me your original face from before you were born'*. In considering this koan, we must explore the thought that the person that we are, was born to fulfil a very specific purpose in our life – a purpose, that perhaps, is not a coincidence in any possible way. However, this koan invites us to inquire more deeply – do we have a purpose that we have not yet managed to discover?

Alex's account is written as a personal 'reflexive' quest – Alex's story is a self-discovery journey that describes his attempt to step outside of himself, walk ten paces forward, and then turn around to face himself and see himself more objectively – without the distortions that our own minds create about who we are. This reflexive inquiry has enabled Alex to be better able to make sense in discovering the purpose he was born to become.

As Alex shares the story of his life's trajectory from this reflexive position, a clarity of his life purpose begins to emerge, and his descriptions of several of his projects help us – as the readers – to better understand 'how' Alex designs the way he does, and 'how' the buildings contribute toward their users receiving benefits from interacting with these buildings.

Alex tells us about his personal 'practices' and his business 'Practice' – in the lower-case instance, he explains that he has a 'contemplative practice', consisting of several regular exercises from a number of disciplinary traditions. In the upper-case instance, Alex describes the business model of his firm – the guild model drawn from the medieval period, based upon a master practitioner who is the teacher and collaborator of apprentices, that is rarely seen in either the management structure or the ethos of most contemporary design firms.

The ancient Greeks coined a word, 'praxis', meaning a lifelong commitment to a form of personal practice that – when followed with rigour and commitment – would lead towards mastery. It is clearly evident, as we follow Alex on his journey, that – indeed – given his focus and attention to his forms of practice, that he has achieved a degree of mastery in his pursuit of praxis and that he is progressing well on his way to even higher degrees.

To read the story of an individual's life is always an opportunity to review our own lives in the light of the story. In the case of reading Alex's story, it is not only an opportunity to learn about Alex and to review our own lives in the light that the story offers – it provides three additional opportunities that are quite unique. The first opportunity is fairly obvious – we can gain insight into how to design more effective environments that contribute towards the improvement of health. The second opportunity offers insights that may enable us to make improvements in our own health and/or quality of life.

However, the brilliant jewel that Alex's story offers us, is a rare opportunity to take a closer look at the events of our own lives – perhaps through a new lens – that may enable us to discover how the Zen koan applies to our lives, and in doing so, provide us with a reflexive insight that enables us to see our own life purpose in a way that we may have never before considered.

*****

I highly commend this book to all readers who share an interest in learning how to further improve health, healthcare, and/or quality of life. Although Alex's account is highly personal and individual to him, it is a valuable reminder to look at our own lives from a wider perspective, as Alex has modelled in his candid description of his life journey.

The pre-Socratic Greeks described this unconcealing of our life purpose as 'aletheia' – an opportunity of self-discovery that is available to all of us, and an exploration that offers profitable findings. I am honoured to have been given the opportunity that my readings of this book have provided to me, and grateful to Alex for the courage that he has demonstrated in his willingness to openly share the story of his life.

Dr. Wayne Ruga
February 2024

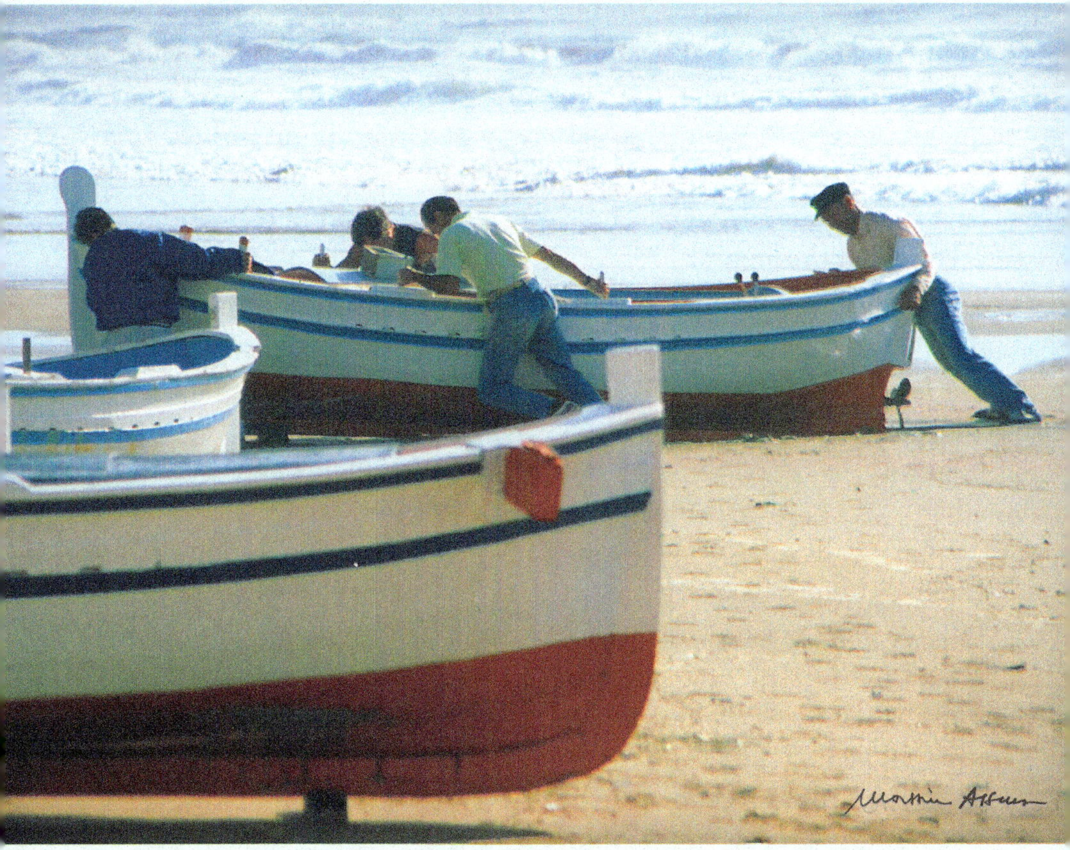

Introduction

This book is dedicated to those who are passionately committed to improving peoples' wellbeing and are interested in learning from my personal journey about the whys and the hows of a transformative design process. A traumatic, past event had a profound impact on my health and thus became my "calling" to improve healthcare environments and people's quality of lives through my designs, exemplified through projects described in the last part of this book.

Being an architect goes beyond the practical requirements of a job description. As I continue to learn how the space designed can influence people's lives, my mission becomes clearer and I realise how the blurred boundaries between work and life offer me endless opportunities to define what makes a fulfilling life. It's a constant and consistent realisation that life offers me all the elements required to design my best project, which can't be judged by its budget and reach, but simply by the awareness that, even if it only positively touches one person's life, I've contributed to their happiness. In addition, throughout the process I've learnt more about how to improve myself, thanks to the relationships developed with the people I've met along the way.

The practical aspect of each project is very important. However, it's the listening process of everybody involved, which is the ultimate key to understanding the meaning of my design response. This feeds my soul and motivates me to search for the next opportunity to influence people's lives. The words of R. Buckminster Fuller, an American architect and prolific writer of the end of the last century, remain close to my quest: *"Never forget that you are one of a kind. Never forget that if there weren't any need for you in all your uniqueness to be on this earth, you wouldn't be here in the first place. And never forget, no matter how overwhelming life's challenges and problems seem to be, that one person can make a difference in the world".*

Several years of study and experience are required to become an architect and by the time we finally gain the qualification, we realise that we've only just started a long apprenticeship! Books and texts on architecture have been written since ancient times and I'm still in the process of reading as many as I can. However, 10 years on from setting up our architectural practice, I now find myself sitting at the same dining table I used at the time of writing my first business plan, with unwavering eagerness, to share what I've learnt through the working of architecture and projects dedicated to people's wellbeing.

I've never been able to keep my books in a pristine condition, as they usually become more a workbook, full of ear marks and highlighting all over, including sketches and annotations. Therefore, at the end of each part in this book, I've deliberately asked a question for you to reflect on and dedicated a blank page for you to add your thoughts.

Throughout the book I use "I/my/me" and "we/our/us" interchangeably. For ease of reference and in general, when I refer to the early concept development of a project, I write for myself and when I refer to our Practice's projects' development throughout the rest of the stages up to completion, I use we/our/us, including the extended client and design team.

I'd like to invite you to share your own information, stories and images on social media platforms (LinkedIn, Facebook, Instagram and X), to become involved in the quest of improving health, healthcare and quality of life, using #ACimprovinghealthbook.

I hope you'll find some useful points from the following pages.

Alessandro Caruso
Beverley, 2024

Background

During one of my trips home to Sicily for the summer holidays someone told me I'd taken the easy option by deciding to move abroad to build my career in architecture, rather than to stay in my native Sicily. Although it hasn't been plain sailing, I have to say that finding a place to flourish has always been my focus, sometimes we need to go and look elsewhere. I have enjoyed every step of the journey so far, with an unshakeable positive outlook.

Soon after graduating, I seized the opportunity to live and work in Madrid for six months, part-funded by a grant received from the European Union. The experience gave me a taste for living in a mind-opening and multicultural environment, much more than my original, small town could offer. There, I met my wife Amelia, who has always influenced my work as a life partner, offering her pragmatic, yet sensitive views on my projects, which have always been important to me. Over the last ten years she has played a critical role in the success of our architectural practice as a co-director: she has strengthened the management of all our operations with a loving interest for what I regard as my hobby and passion with a complementarity of observations.

I'm fortunate that my work allows me to travel a fair bit and I find each trip filled with rewarding new interests, which generates new questions and observations.

Going back to being told I'd taken the easy option, it had never occurred to me that there was an easy option! I just felt the need to find my space where I could nurture the meaning of my profession, working on my resilience, the way I came to understand that my father had done in his early days.

I worked in the family architecture business my father founded in our hometown, Pozzallo, for as long as I can remember. Whilst studying Architecture, I'd often meet people who had worked for my father in the early days of his contractor enterprise, who remembered me as a child arriving with my father on a construction site. They remembered me playing with the mounds of sands used to make cement mix for construction. This would certainly be frowned upon today, if I did such a thing with my own children, as it would probably be in violation of Health and Safety legislation, yet it nurtured my early interest for the industry.

My father's office was above our apartment in Pozzallo overlooking the seafront. I used to enjoy the mesmerising views the horizon offered regardless of the season, dreaming of what was beyond, while I was learning the ropes of my future career. In my early days as the office junior, I was sent on errands for anything the office staff required. The rest of the time, I spent sifting through the endless numbers of books and journals populating the office shelves, answering calls and learning from conversations amongst more senior colleagues.

I was very young and I hadn't yet figured out the career I wanted. Through the little time I was able to spend with my father, I sensed that architecture required an around the clock commitment, which was very contrasting compared to the regular working hours my mother did as an Italian teacher. I always knew my mother would support any decision I would take and still does today. However, my interest in architecture remained a fascinating presence which was difficult to ignore because my father would often try to encourage me to choose the profession he loved; for him it was his childhood dream, yet for me, I wasn't sure I felt the same. I didn't know any different as I'd been born into the architecture industry, experiencing it every day and I hated the idea of having to choose a career just to please my father or because it was an obvious and easy choice.

The critical time for a decision came as soon as I finished high school. Throughout the 5 years of predominantly Science and Maths based studies, my quest for discovering what was beyond the immediate horizon intensified, inspired by Philosophy and English studies and movies such as "Top Gun" and "An Officer and a Gentleman", which sparked a determination to try and become a pilot. At the time the main route was via the RAF equivalent "Accademia Aereounautica di Pozzuoli", where I failed the selection criteria on the first day of medical examinations because I was too tall for a Jet fighter cockpit! Disappointed with this result, I tried to become a helicopter pilot, approaching the Navy equivalent "Accademia Navale di Livorno", where this time I managed to spend five days after passing the initial selection. It was an eye-opening experience! I always knew I could be self-disciplined, however I realised that with my free spirit and ready-to-challenge approach to life, I would have struggled to flourish within the strict discipline of a military life. I like to think that I learnt to fly through the working of architecture instead.

When I started at the Faculty of Architecture in Palermo, from the early assignments and subjects it was obvious to me that I had been wasting my time searching for Pandora in other places, when it had always been clearly in front of my eyes. My university years flew by, with interesting theoretical studies and practical projects experiences alongside my father. We would often discuss the same critical question: "what constitutes architecture as a "state of the art" in what we design every day?", a question that I still ask myself about any of my projects.

Towards the end of my university course however, a serious motorbike accident forced me to postpone my studies for over a year. As painful as the experience and recovery was, it became a lightbulb moment and the catalyst for my career.

I spent six weeks confined to a hospital bed in an Orthopaedic Traumatology Centre in Palermo. I was on a 6-bedded unit and the patients would regularly change, as most were transferred to other wards. I could hear ambulances arriving every few minutes most days and nights, making it difficult to rest and recover. Also, I had no idea how many other bedded units there were along the corridor or indeed how big the hospital was. I recall that my bed was near the corridor, with the door always open so that nurses could easily monitor my convalescence. I still remember the intensity of some admissions, particularly overnight, when I would try to sit up or at least crane my neck to see what was happening.

Until my accident, I'd been busy living life to the full and was always involved in something, be it studying, working, sports or social life. The long weeks constrained to a hospital bed stopped all that but revealed a silver lining. I developed empathic skills I didn't know I had, sparking a real interest in healing architecture. After I eventually left the hospital, I still had to go back for other diagnostics and medical procedures and every time I'd ask the doctors and nurses insights into their profession.

Not much has changed since, if anything my curiosity continued to grow because thankfully, health and social care is a sector that offers endless opportunities for research and development. Upon completion of a project that has given me lots to consider, I know that the next project, which appears to be similar on the surface, will be completely different because there are different people with different requirements. Also, the time that elapses between one project and the next, reveals the latest innovations to consider, making it a totally unique project.

What I viewed as *only a job* in my early years, has not just become a love, like my father always used to say, but my true passion. This comes with a mission to improve peoples' lives with the integrity of buildings that can combine purpose and beauty; I share the knowledge acquired after each experience either via publications or speaking at conferences, along with what I hope to be my first book capturing my journey along the way. It has offered me the opportunity to visit places and build stimulating relationships and experiences associated with different projects, not to mention the admiration for the people who work in any care environment. Irrespective of how great a building looks, it wouldn't be fit for purpose without the engine that keeps it moving.

My architecture journey has been guided by principles learnt along the way in my contemplative practice on how to live and design a more fulfilling life based on five main elements: firstly, spirituality to find my mission in this life; secondly, an apprenticeship through the practice of what I learn every day; thirdly, an awareness that I need look after myself; fourthly, an awareness that I need to look after people and the community around me and finally, the importance of nurturing harmonious relationships with people and our planet.

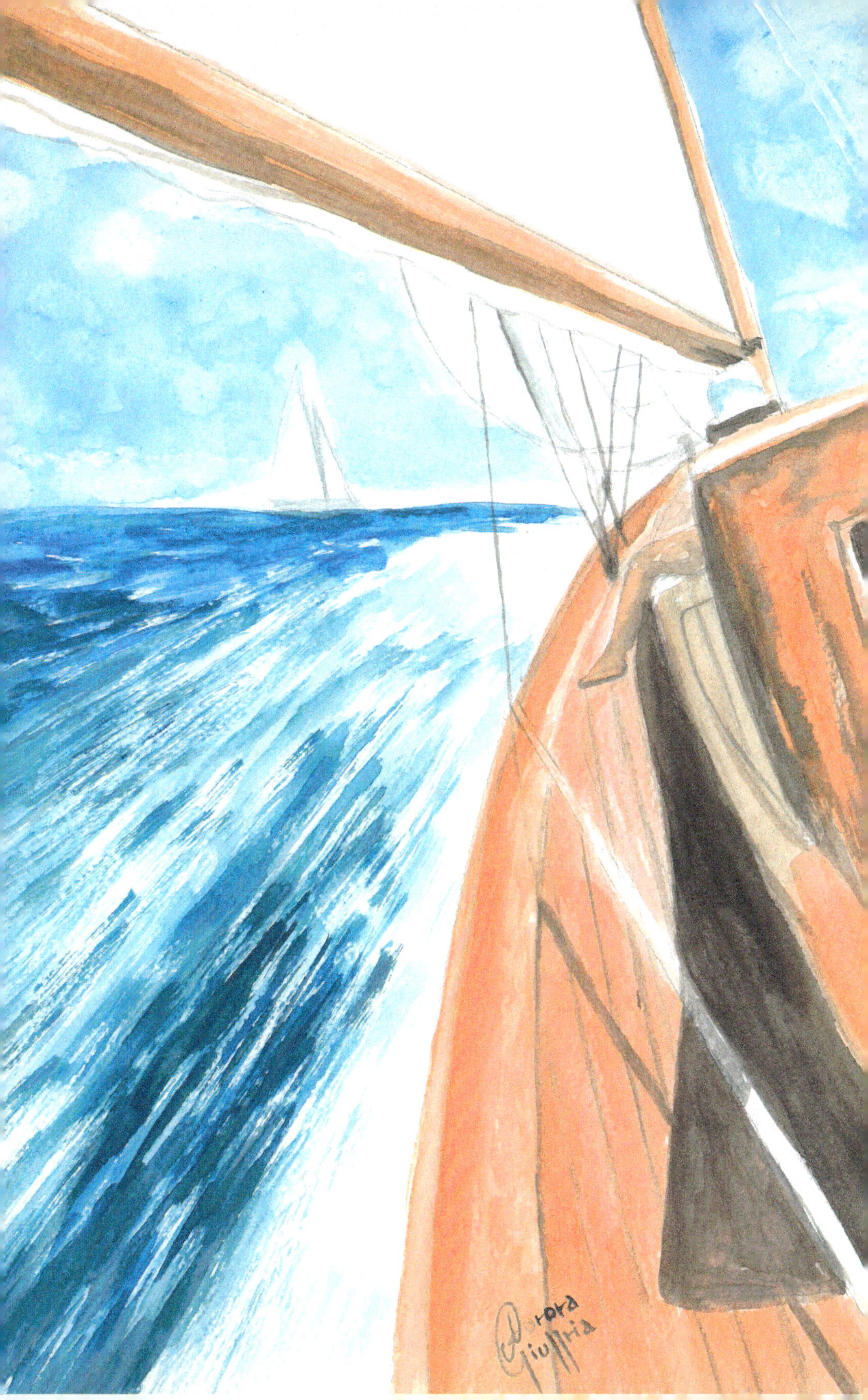

Existential Context

Life Journey

"A wave is never in isolation and you can't look at one wave without bearing in mind the complex features that concur in shaping it and the other, equally complex ones that the wave itself generates."

Mr. Palomar, Italo Calvino

Born

I grew up in Pozzallo, a small town and commercial port in the south of Sicily, built around the imposing presence of the Cabrera watchtower. Built in the early 15th century, the tower used to defend Pozzallo from pirate attacks and soon became the heart of the original village settlement for soldiers and fishermen. I'm not aware of any immediate family of fishermen; however I've always felt a strong connection with this primordial way of life and the idea of venturing out in search for food.

The province of Ragusa is part of the Val di Noto and is recognised as a UNESCO area for Baroque architecture; it was during this period that the area was almost entirely rebuilt after a particularly destructive earthquake that ruined the area in 1608.

Sicily, I love this land and couldn't be prouder of its place in history. At times, you can see the night sky lit up by the eruptions of Europe's highest active volcano, Etna and hear the thundering that comes from the centre of the earth. Sicily boasts a countryside with colours ranging from ochre in the freshly harvest fields in summer to vivid green in winter. There is also a sea of various colour shades, from green to cobalt blue, depending on the coastline that presents alternating rocky cliffs or fine sand and pebbled beaches. There is a sea full of marine life which easily changes its nature from angry and wavy during stormy weather to calm and welcoming during sunny days.

Sicilians have a very distinct character compared to mainland Italians, most notably they are very laid back and relaxed about most things. Sicily is a melting pot of cultures and races which has left a variety of legacies in history, art and architecture, cooking recipes and traditions. Its strategic location at the centre of the Mediterranean Sea made Sicily a crossroads for many cultures, including Phoenicians, Greeks, Arabs, Normans, Romans, British, and French. Norman palaces, Roman ruins, and Greek temples are scattered throughout the cities, rolling hillsides and beautiful coasts of the island as a legacy to the vast history of visitors and conquerors.

The Sicilian language is very different to Italian and incorporates a blend of words from Arabic, Hebrew, Byzantine, and Norman influencing our unique culture, yet like many Sicilians what I dislike about this land is that it's still best known for the mafia, which hampers the entrepreneurial spirit of its people. I love to return on holidays to see family and friends, yet when it comes to my work, Sicily is a place that sadly, I'm happy to have left behind. Coming from an island full of contradictions, I learnt early enough to dream of faraway imaginary places where the grass is greener. Although the grass isn't always greener as first naively imagined it has given me an understanding that it's simply a question of perspective.

I lived most of my early life in Pozzallo in apartments, usually in front of the sea. The sea and beach have always been a huge part of my life since the womb. My mother tells me that when I was a very young child, during the summers at the beach, she would let me wander about and would often find me playing with another family's children under a beach umbrella, before moving on to the next.

I'm not sure how happy I was as a child. I was curious, perhaps disobedient, and often reprimanded. To this day I have few distinct memories of that period. On one of the photos of me at that time, my expression is melancholic. Perhaps it was due to the learning environment which I found neither interesting nor stimulating and I would've rather been elsewhere.

My first school was a building from the second half of the 18th Century. It had a main door which led to an intimidating atrium with a central staircase which felt much bigger than me. The classroom I shared with another 30 children had only one window, high ceilings and grey walls; almost as if it had been designed to quash any children's spirit rather than to inspire them to thrive.

It was a real contrast to the views from the apartment where I lived. At the time, my father had a construction business and used to design and build blocks of flats. He used to reserve the top floor for us until he sold all the apartments and moved on to the next building approaching completion. In our first apartment, there weren't any doors, so it was an ideal playground for a young child and my mother says that I used to like running from one room to another without any obstacles.

We had a 360 degree terrace and what I remember most, apart from the views of the sea and the coast, was the sunlight and its differing reflections on the sea depending on the time of day or the view of the port with boats coming and going. The large glass windows were a constant subliminal invitation to the life outdoors.

If it's true that our lives are influenced predominantly by our childhoods, I'm sure that my love for the fluidity of spaces and using the exterior as an extension of the interior, comes from those early experiences.

The sea was mesmerising to watch at any time of the year nurturing my early contemplative nature and love for being out amongst nature. Also, the beach was my big three-dimensional canvas, as it was something I could interact with to make sandcastles or simply to observe the organic shapes of the dunes, trying to understand the forces that the wind or the rough sea had used to form them. After a storm the beach would become an open biology lab, hosting all sorts of sea creatures, with interesting geometries and colourful shells, trapped by the algae brought ashore by the rough sea. Even today, particularly during stormy weather, I often go to a beach in Hornsea, not far from where I live in Beverley. I enjoy seeing inclement conditions, experiencing the force of nature, particularly at sea, it energises me and helps me put things into perspective.

My mother has always been my anchor, she's always been present when I've needed her, despite my long periods of silence during some stages of my life. When I was a child, she would teach me to be sensitive to other people's feelings and respectful to everyone, but to fiercely defend myself when necessary if people took advantage of my friendly nature. As an Italian teacher amongst my friends, she had the reputation of being outspoken, strong, and authoritative yet inspiring and motivational; as a mother she's always had the softest of hearts, being loving and infinitely supportive, despite her tough matriarchal image to other people. My mother has always encouraged me to follow my heart even when perhaps she completely disagreed with my choices. She's always been a balancing force ready to offer her perspective if I want an alternative view. She's always motivated me to do better than before without comparing myself to others. From my mother, I've learnt the importance of family values and care.

My father has a completely different personality, he's always been patient, diplomatic and more inclined to offer a listening ear, without comment. Throughout my life, I believe I've probably learnt a lot more from what he's held back from saying than from what he has actually said.

As a self-made man with a laser-focused vision for what he wanted to achieve in life, his experience of childhood was typical of the children who'd lived during the second world war and its aftermath. He spent his childhood working hard to contribute to his family upbringing. He still describes those years as a period when they had nothing, yet they didn't lack anything. His childhood was influenced by the stories his father would tell him about the war and the images of the early movies that arrived in the village. He struggled to understand my childhood apparent lack of interest in his profession, and it wasn't until I started following him in his work that our relationship improved. Nowadays, he tells me that he understands that I was absorbing the architectural environment with a rather more detached approach to his. We spent more time together during my adult life when I started working alongside him than we did playing together; until I was old enough to play tennis or table tennis.

My father was my first Art teacher at school (amongst the several hats he was able to wear at the same time), and I'm sure I was a tough kid to teach because my thoughts would easily be transported outside the classroom. I'm still the same now, when not fully engaged in a subject, I drift off thinking of something else more enticing. He loves Art in all forms and was a teacher well-respected by students and other teachers for his passionate lessons.

He's always expected more of me regardless of how much I could give and this was often highlighted as not necessarily fair by some of my school friends. From his approach to teaching, I learnt to motivate myself to do better than before for my own sake. Perhaps indirectly, he also taught me the importance of objectively challenging judgement and questioning the reasons behind. I'm sure his best intention was to build confidence and interest in my learning, however perhaps he overcompensated in trying to prove that he was an objective teacher in his assessment of my abilities. Maybe this was one of my first encounters with life questions at crossroads: Was I a loser? Should I rebel or embrace the challenge? I was unhindered by internal conflicts and dare I say I thrived under the adversity my father's method. Over the years I worked hard without discounting his views and trusted myself even when people doubted me, expressing myself through the creative work I produced without too much concern for the teachers' assessments. I would accept their feedback and move on.

Thanks to my father, I learnt the love for architecture and the importance of creativity in everyday life: everything is design. I learnt to like drawing and particularly sketching to lose myself in thought whilst capturing the perspective of what I was looking at, it is a process I liken to an exercise in awareness. I can be selective about what to keep in my sketching, with ever-deepening layers of complexity and what to omit.

I only met my paternal grandmother when I was first born and have no memory of her as she died soon after; my paternal grandfather was great fun. He had built and set up the first cinema in Pozzallo with his brothers and he would often take me there. I had access to anywhere in the building and the room I always found the most intriguing was the projector room, which you could access via a hidden set of stairs. I always felt I had a very privileged access to a special room, that in truth was a very small and practical room with just about enough space for the projector operator and storage for the film reels. I still describe the time with my grandfather very much like the childhood of young Toto in the film "Nuovo Cinema Paradiso" by Giuseppe Tornatore. Unfortunately, my grandfather died when I was still very young and our times together at the cinema soon came to an end.

My maternal grandparents lived in Palermo and we rarely saw them until the summer, when they would spend it at home with us.

When we moved to the apartment block where my mother still lives, along came my sister Marcella and eventually my brother Enrico. We were all very close in age and childhood started to become more fun. We had a dedicated playroom where we could do whatever we wanted, like drawing on the walls or playing with a heap of Lego to build all sorts of elaborate constructions.

When my parents were at work, we would often spend time with

Nonna Muriana. She was not related to us, but she lived in the same block of apartments. After the death of her husband, she decided to move from Bologna to our town and soon became our surrogate Grandma. She was the first in the condominium to have a colour television and she was happy to invite all the children in the block to watch TV programs with her. Meanwhile she used to love playing cards with a couple of pensioners from the condominium and I recall using the cards they were not playing with to explore card castle solutions. Nowadays multi-generational housing and opportunities to bring different generations together to help one another is a big topic, yet back then it all felt like the most natural way of living.

Nonna Muriana was with us until I finished university and in the latter stages of her life, through my work, I eventually recognised that she started showing certain symptoms of Alzheimer's: being forgetful or drifting in and out of cognition. I remember once I went to visit her; she looked directly at a chicken pox scar on my forehead and asked if I had been shot! Considering what Sicily is best known for, it may have made sense to her. She lived happily in her home almost until the end.

Over recent years I've been exploring ways to recreate a model of multi-generational living for families in the United Kingdom, be it for living or older age care environment.

A family business

As the family grew, we used to spend our Sundays in what we used to call "la campagna", a rural plot of land. In its origin it was rather a barren and rocky plot of land with a steep sloping ground which was used by my father's construction company to store construction materials.

There wasn't much more other than a small rural building used for storage and a few old Carob trees under which we would eat what my mother had prepared at home. I used to love spending time there climbing the trees and it felt like freedom compared to the week at school.

One of the Carob trees had branches that were quite low down and a couple of them were at approximately the same level, so I figured out that I could make my climbing experience rather more comfortable if I could build some form of a terrace; I used to spend time rummaging through the materials stored to see what I could make use of. Slowly but surely, I started borrowing some timber planks, generally used for scaffolding, to carry them under the trees and eventually lift them over the branches. It wasn't too long before I completed a rudimentary terrace made of timber planks balanced amongst the branches and it became the place where I used to proudly invite my siblings, cousins and friends who came to visit. It was a space generally reserved for the youngsters where the adults wouldn't normally venture. In hindsight it was a bit of a health and safety nightmare that only the most intrepid of us dared to visit.

On completing the last of the block of apartments and having graduated in Architecture, my father decided to close the construction company and dedicate his time to what he enjoyed most, designing for others without the headache of always having to wear a commercial hat.

"Campagna" started to evolve into a country house and from week to week for months and years afterwards, each Sunday I could see the transformative progress made in the formation of land terraces to make the land more usable, where I came up with new games with what I could find. One of my favourites was to cycle from the top of the hilly grounds down to a flat area of concrete where I'd arranged some planks to perform bike jumps and I thoroughly enjoyed these activities on the edge of safety, pushing myself through the latest daring thrill.

Once the formation of the land terraces were ready, the construction of rooms, some with fireplaces began. I became even more interested in understanding the space under construction and its use and construction methods. When I was allowed (I don't think I was even ten years old) in the summer I used to like joining the block layers and carpenters to dig or carry materials for them, whilst learning the culture of a building site and its construction methods.

I still love to visit construction sites to verify ideas explored on paper and visually monitor the progress since my last visit. I enjoy the banter with the construction team about certain design details and how to improve them, it makes me proud of being part of the process. Writing today about those early formative years makes me realise the profound effect such a childhood has had on me in understanding the culture of being an architect, beyond its job description. I still see architecture as a miracle, a transformative art I can't help but love for its esoteric and magical process, teaming up with mother nature and what she has to offer, seeing possibilities where others can't and transforming all of this into a building that touches peoples' lives. I've learnt that every child is born with more than four hundred psychological traits which emerge during its life, and I like to think I've been blessed with being born into a family where the culture of making something from nothing has run through our veins for generations. In the brief exchanges about his memories, my father describes my great grandfather, who I never met, as an eclectic character who, with no formal education, was equally masterful in the art of designing and building houses and furniture, not only conceiving their design but

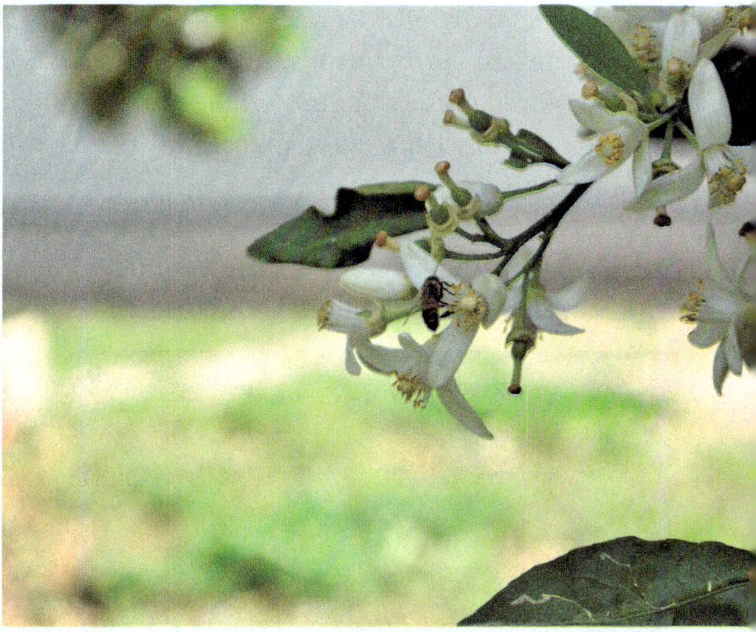

executing it practically, with the use of his own hands.

My grandfather, along with his brothers, didn't have a better education than my great grandfather, yet he was no less entrepreneurial. During the hardships of the war, he saw the potential in an old and ruined warehouse, to restore it and convert it into what became the first cinema in Pozzallo, offering time for information and entertainment to its population. My father was one of the first to achieve a diploma and a degree in the family.

There are many of my father's projects that I like, but "campagna" is by far the one I love the most, it's not only the sentimental value, but I also enjoyed observing the whole transformative process from a humble store to what it is today, with its organic evolution around the natural context.

The crafting of "campagna" is still evolving and remains my father's favourite playground for experimentation. I still spend time with him discussing his latest ideas on how to make best use of a certain material in a certain part of the house, which is now a holiday home for guests from around the world, who want to experience this small corner of Sicily.

When there aren't any guests, it's my favourite place to indulge in the solitude of my walking meditation amongst the trees. It's given me the understanding that as an art, architecture isn't a finished process that you can freeze at the conditions of its origin. The buildings I design offer people a similar immersive experience and as an architect, I feel the responsibility to listen to the building users' needs, to respond with an evolving relationship with the space, which in many ways reflects the developing human relationships inside.

The process behind each project becomes a new learning adventure with infinite, varying opportunities offered by the sensitive perception of the context, the materials and ultimately, the people at the heart of their community. It goes beyond the technical and legal knowledge

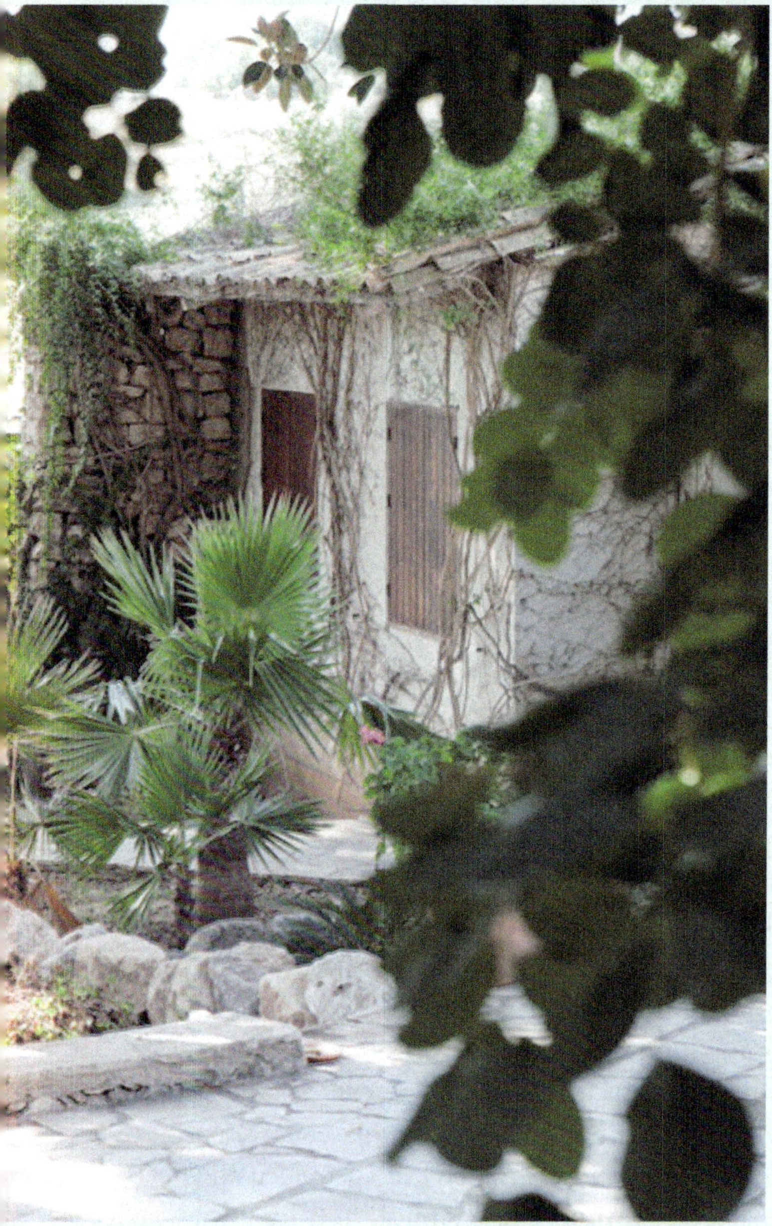

required, which is critical to support the symbolism behind the initial concept offered; as an architect, above all, I have the responsibility for the social impact and emotions generated by our buildings.

"Campagna" was not simply a place where we would spend the summer months, it also became our "virtual office" during those times. Our usual architectural office was at the top of block of apartments where we used to live during the winter months, but like most family businesses, work discussions never stopped there; they would follow us wherever we went, particularly when my sister Marcella completed her degree in structural engineering in Florence and returned to Sicily.

Marcella's addition to the team created a new dynamic and the discussions about design had an embedded structural practicality from the outset of every project. What I loved about her input was that the structural design process didn't start when the architects had finished, it became an iterative process of testing ideas with energy, of which she had plenty, without losing the speed required to meet any deadlines.

Multi-disciplinary teamwork is still both a value and a process at the heart of my architectural practice, where the emphasis on whose idea is moving forward is left behind in favour of the idea that has been challenged and tested the most: the initial sketch is designed, tested, discussed, and reinterpreted until it is agreed by all parties to be the design that satisfies all project requirements. The learning curve behind every project is exponential, particularly where we have had the opportunity to experiment with the use of new construction technologies and or materials for a new type of building service.

University

I believe life is about understanding your options. Having tried out two military academies which didn't live up to my expectations and explored the opportunity of studying in Florence, I decided to register in the Faculty of Architecture in Palermo to give it a try. If I didn't like it, my father told me that the alternative was to start working on one of his construction sites.

I loved my life in Palermo where I was surrounded by the most spectacular, creative and immersive environment I could wish for. I just needed to let my senses take it all in.

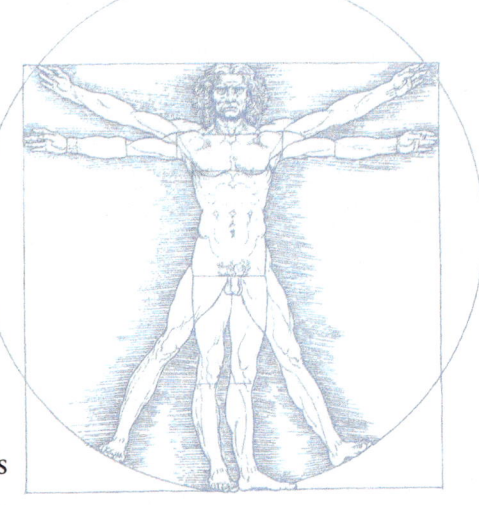

From the very first lesson on the Roman Architect and Engineer Vitruvius's principles of *firmitas* (strength), *utilitas* (utility), and *venustas* (beauty) reflected in much of Roman Architecture, it became clear to me the role that Italian design had had in the national consciousness and history. Everything felt familiar about this learning environment, I could instinctively understand it and felt that I'd wasted my time in stubbornly trying to follow an adolescent dream of flying that was never in my genes. The first year was particularly inspiring, we learnt about ideal human proportions delving into the study of Leonardo Da Vinci's Vitruvian Man inscribed in a circle and a square. The idea of the exercise was relatively simple, we needed to use our own body to replicate Leonardo's image. However, the significance of the image became more and more clear to me in years to come; I started to understand how the world surrounding human beings relates to such proportions adopting the φ golden ratio (present in nature) and ultimately the importance of creating buildings in relation to the people who live and work there. I went on to study the foundation rules of classical decorative styles such as Doric and Corinthian in contrast with the minimalist school of modern architects such Walter Gropius or Mies van der Rohe. I immediately embraced the research for the essence in the work of Mies and his philosophy of "Less is more". To deepen my understanding of it, I developed a study of axonometric views of the "the house with three courts" to visualise the correspondence between the voids in the roof opening to the sky and the corresponding courts. The tall perimeter walls maximised the use of the plot of land all year around whilst retaining the privacy for the residents of the house. Life around a court is a simple concept that I'm still exploring in my work today.

I used to prefer the building design courses where I could use my sketching to interpret abstract concepts, but what particularly fed my design vocabulary was everything that fascinated me on my walks through the streets of Palermo between my student accommodation and the faculty. As I walked, looking up most of the time, I absorbed the difference in styles between different buildings and parts of the old city. As I passed through the old markets, I dived into the experience of the calls of market traders and admired the colours, textures and essences of the food displayed. I likened it to a daily performing theatre or a living artwork capturing all your senses at once. Since then I regard an immersive experience as the main quality of the space.

The years passed rather quickly between studying and socialising with the friends I shared my apartment with. We were all architecture students at different stages of our careers. Those ahead of me, such as Ferdinando, were happy to share their experiences. Looking back, the environment we were living in was just as creative as it was fun, creating wonderful memories and long-lasting friendships to this day.

I can't say that I recall one subject better than another. I used to do well in design subjects but didn't achieve top marks until the end of my studies; the Professors would often mark down my projects because they considered them overly pragmatic for that stage of my career, when imagination and creativity was what they wanted to see. Needless to say, this frustrated me with a dull ache, since I was used to working alongside my father, where I had to have a pragmatic approach as well as providing creative design solutions.

This feedback fuelled a sympathy in me for the structural engineering design subjects where I did rather well using my intuition for the structural system design, more than the accuracy of my hand calculations.

What university did for me was to open my mind with ever thought-provoking books and a design vocabulary beyond anything I had seen until starting the first year, learning about architecture around the world which I longed to experience. To this day when we travel on holiday, I always research what sightseeing I can fit in, to the joy of my family!

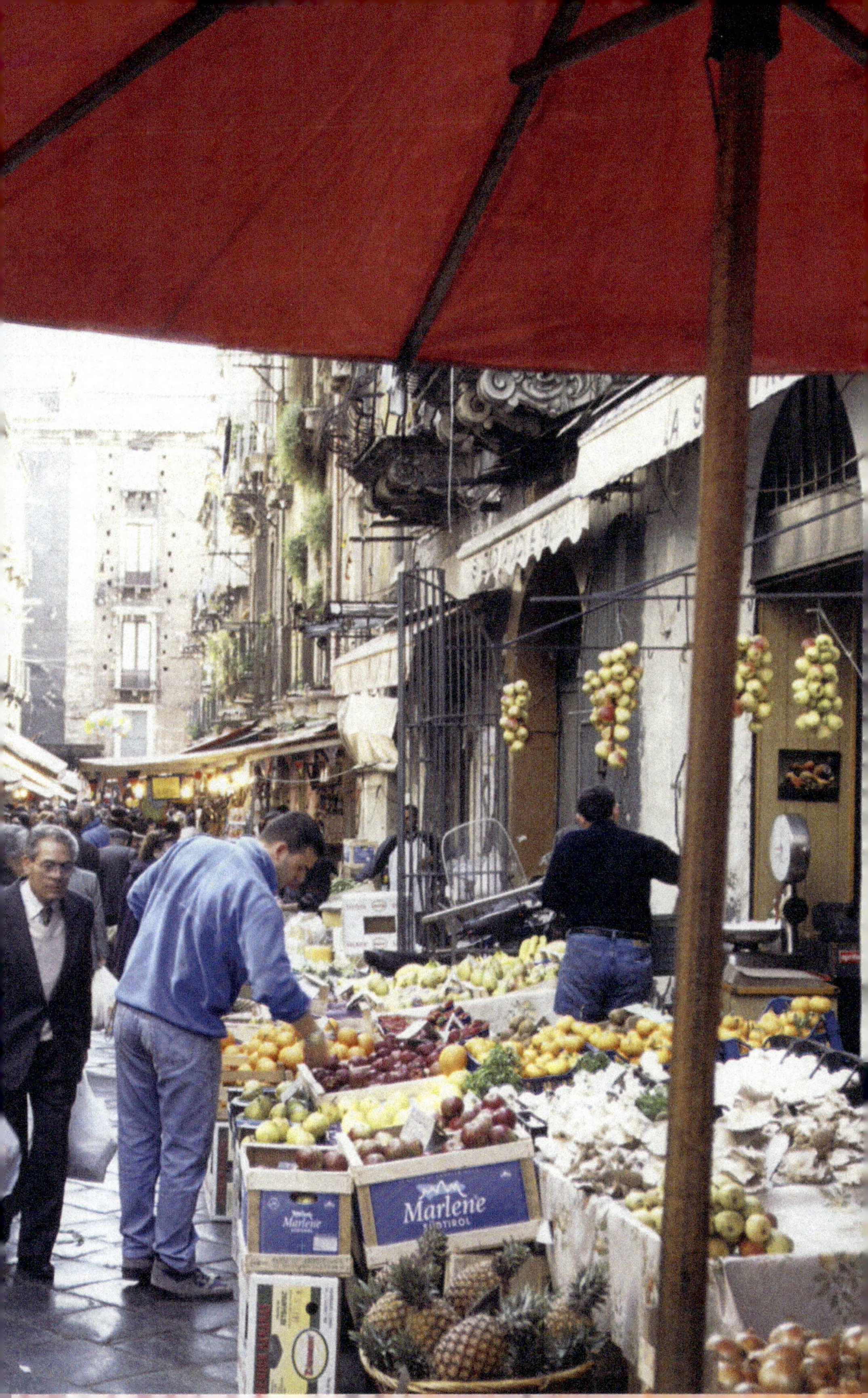
Marlene

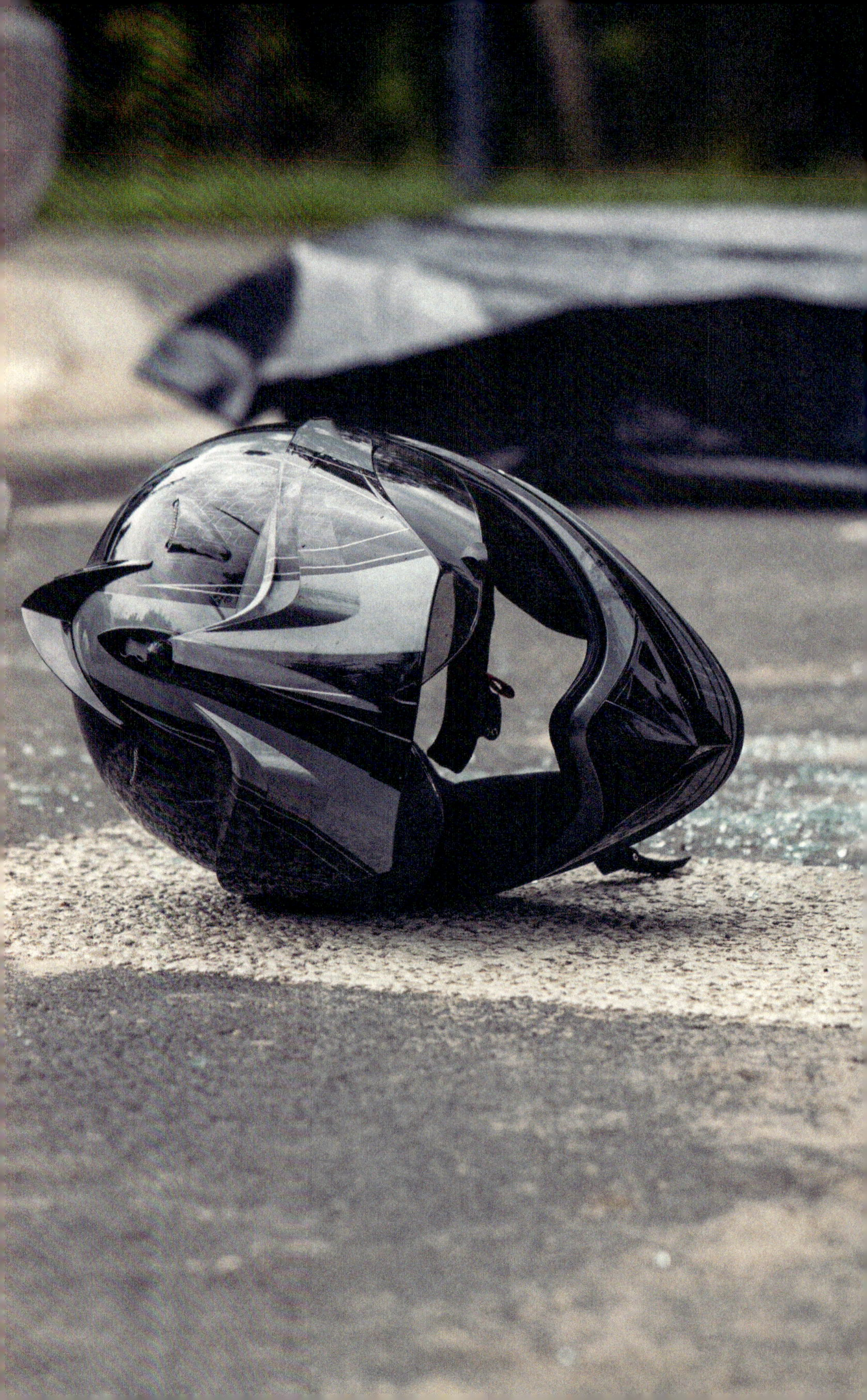

Accident

I opened my eyes and I was on the ground unable to feel anything nor understand why I was there. Suddenly, I felt a shooting pain coming from my right arm and tried to reach out with my left. In a matter of split seconds, the pain from my lower body hit me, but this time I couldn't reach or move, so I remained paralysed on the floor, my body on the warm tarmac of the road and my legs over the kerb. The pain was excruciating and I couldn't move my legs. There were people all around me, some asking who to call and some trying to comfort me, reassuring me that the ambulance was on the way. I realised that this time, it wasn't one of my usual falls on a motocross circuit.

I didn't want my family to know, so I gave my student accommodation telephone number, in the hope that one of my flatmates could come. I don't recall much of the journey in the ambulance as I must have been sedated.

My first memory was outside the operating theatre, I was in pain again, so I guess the sedation was wearing off, but Antonio, my Uncle Bruno and Aunt Eleonora were there. As I recognised them, I asked if they knew the extent of my injuries but they didn't know. I asked them not to tell my parents as I didn't want them to worry.

By the time I came round in my hospital bedroom, my parents were already there. I thought it was strange because the town where my parents lived was over 4 hours away from the hospital in Palermo. The operation had been a lengthy one and my mum told me that my right hip was broken in several pieces, which had been put together, my right knee ligament had been rebuilt and the good news was that my right arm had only been dislocated and didn't require further operations.

Following my second operation, I spent the next six weeks strapped to my bed with my leg in traction. My restless nature had been grounded to a halt with a grim outlook in front of me. My studies at university, the nightlife and friendships appeared to be all wiped out for the foreseeable future.

Needless to say, a lot of questions started to pop into my head about what would've happened if I hadn't taken my motorbike to Palermo against my parents' judgement, or if on that day, instead of going to study at a friend's house on my motorbike, I'd stayed at home? But also, what would've happened if, on that very warm ninth day of April in 1994, I'd not worn my helmet, as I usually didn't? My helmet had cracked on impact and had to be removed by the ambulance nurses. I still remember the persistent headaches that followed my admission into hospital and the need to close my eyes and shut down while my family tried to keep me awake for fear of serious implications from any brain injury caused by the crash.

I was riding along the roads of Palermo in the early afternoon, when most people in our culture take a lunchtime nap and I felt on top of the world. I can't deny that I may have been speeding a little. As I rode, I could see a crossroads a few hundred metres ahead, with a secondary road, where a car was stationary; I slowed down slightly, then, believing the driver was waiting for me to pass, carried on full throttle. It was a matter of seconds before I hit the car at full speed and I can only remember trying to avoid it by turning towards the left.

Many said it was a miracle I was still alive and that without the helmet, the 9-metre flight and impact with the ground, could've had a very different ending. What was just a casual decision that afternoon to go out on my motorbike, had such a drastic effect on my life's direction. I've never cared too much about the past as my focus has always been in front of me, but this was different. What would my life have been like if I'd not experienced the accident? I'd endured previous motorbike accidents during my endurance and motocross circuits practice, which had resulted in various scrapes and aches and pains, but in comparison to this, merely felt like being prodded with toothpicks. Was this a more direct message to warn me to stop what I was doing?

After the last operation the surgeon came to see me and reassured me that I wasn't paralysed and the reason I couldn't move both legs, was because my right leg was dislocated and its location prevented my other leg from moving. That was a huge relief and I remember feeling exhilarated as he delivered the news. He also told me not to worry too much about being in traction; this was only a temporary measure for 6 weeks to ensure my pelvis reconstruction had sufficient space to heal within the joint. He went on to say that they'd done everything they could during both operations, however it was very likely that I would limp for the rest of my life. I thanked him and his team with the enthusiasm of a child and assured him that I would do my best to recover and get back on my feet as near as possible to how I was before.

The following weeks proved to be rather testing for my usual positive outlook, as the pain was unbearable and continuous, preventing me from sleeping or simply resting. Despite being dosed up to the maximum on painkillers, I begged the nurses for more at every rota change.

I was in a room with five other people and my bed was near the door so that nurses could easily monitor my convalescence as they cared for other patients. Natural light was limited to a single window on the opposite side of the room so I couldn't see any interesting views outside, only the blue sky in the distance, which became my only ray of hope. I used to ask my mother to tell me what she could see when she came to visit, to keep me entertained.

The room surfaces included terrazzo tiles and plastered painted walls and ceilings and some of the fellow patients with whom I shared the room tended to snore rather loudly! The room finishes proved to be an ideal ground for noise reverberation, which didn't help my already unstable sleeping pattern. My only respite was to use the white ceiling as a blank canvas for my imagination.

With the room door predominantly left open day and night, it was difficult not to hear the intensity of new admissions, some of which would end up on my bedded unit. Stimulating, but not for the right reasons!

From time-to-time friends would come and visit me particularly at the weekend when the atmosphere would change to an entertaining

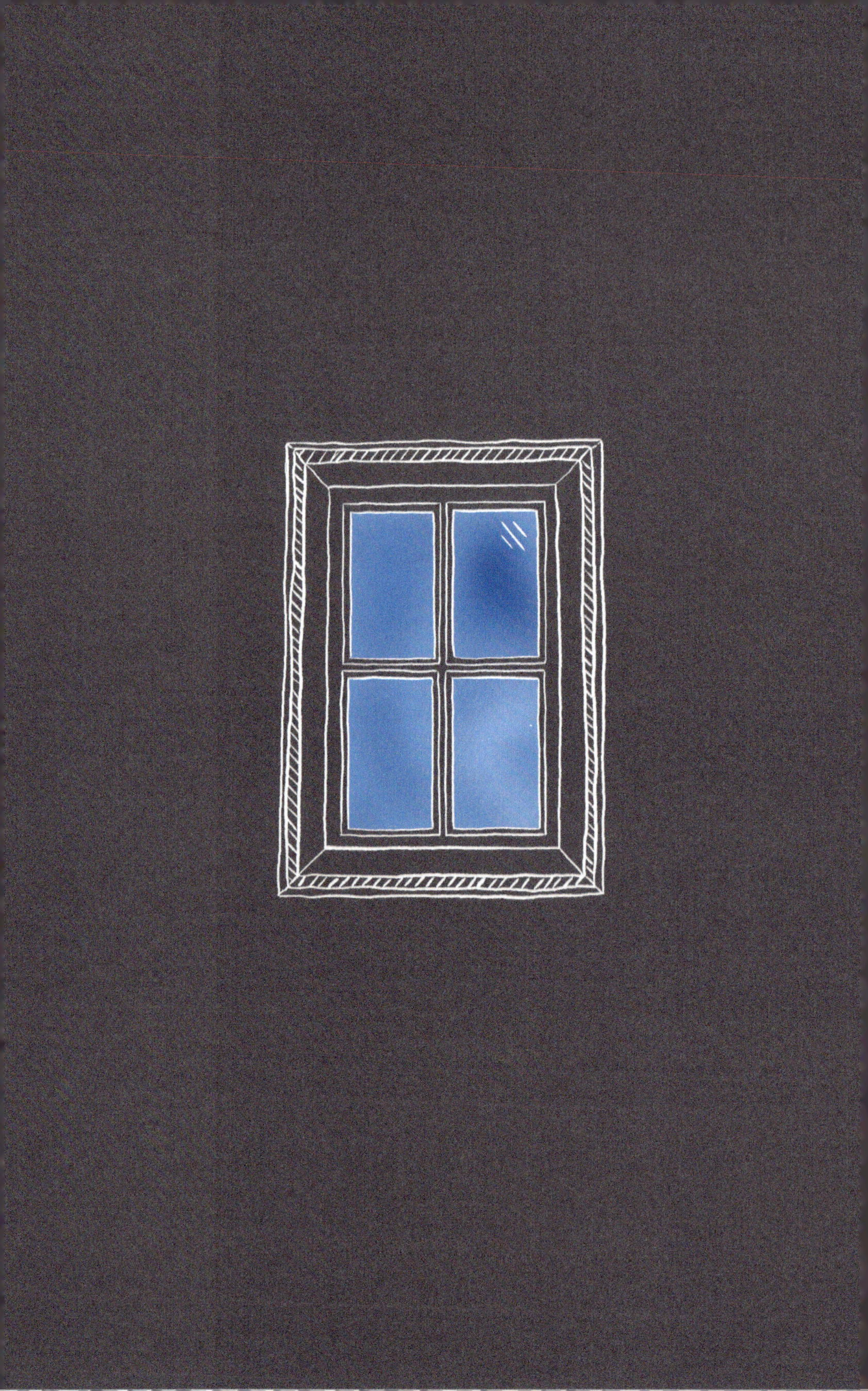

one for the full room; my mum would tirelessly come to see me almost every day and fill me in on the latest, just to distract me from my pain.

When she wasn't there, I'd get to know fellow patients and their families; some of them knew I couldn't move, so they'd come and sit near my bed to exchange stories about why they were there. Some of the stories were remarkably like mine, yet others, particularly for the older generation, were due to falls associated to old age. I remember a man in his early thirties, in a wheelchair, who'd often come to see me from the other end of the corridor. He shared with me, in vivid detail how he'd tried to kill himself at least four times in various ways, due to depression. The reason he was in a wheelchair was because he had failed in his latest attempt to commit suicide by jumping off a building. He had survived and was paralysed from the waist down. He reminded me of a junior school friend who had killed himself during high school; when we were children we often used to study or play together but we'd chosen different high schools and I often wonder if he would still be here today, if he'd had a listening ear at hand. You never know what's going on in other people's lives.

I have always been outgoing, perhaps preferring a superficial party to any deep and intense atmosphere. However, during that time, forced in a perpetually reflective and supine position, I started to develop a disposition for reflective practice. I'd notice how people felt at a deeper level, not just physically but also psychologically. From my bed I'd distract myself from my pain by observing other people's feelings and offering a listening ear when they wanted. I remember my mother asking me why I was always happy to listen to so many sad stories when I was visibly in pain most of the time and my answer was often that my pain was merely physical and I just needed to wait for it to pass as my body healed. However, it was a very different pain from the one I could sense from others like the guy in the wheelchair, I could perceive his struggle in trying to live with such unhappiness. That instinctive empathic response drove me to learn about my feelings and emotions more deeply and how to put them aside to be able to focus on what affects other people's feelings and how they perceive the world.

The end of the six weeks finally arrived and I realised that during that time I'd read several books, allowing me to travel in space and time despite the physical constraints of a hospital bed. The surgeons removed the weights and the spindle through the bottom of my thigh bone and I was finally allowed to leave hospital, with a reminder that my recovery was still ongoing: I needed to spend at least six more weeks laying on a bed before moving to a wheelchair for another six weeks.

By the time I was getting around on crutches, I realised that after four and a half months without the need for them, the muscles in both of my legs had weakened. When I first stood up, I had no sense of balance and had completely forgotten how to move one leg in front of the other. I had to re-learn how to balance on my feet and to walk. The simple action of standing and moving one foot in front of the other required my full concentration, as it didn't come naturally to me anymore because neural pathways needed to be rewired. It felt like I had another lifetime of restricted moves in front of me. However, my physiotherapist told me that I could start swimming as soon as I was in a wheelchair. Like most people who live near the sea, I loved swimming and had always enjoyed a good swim. So, in the months to come, as I improved and was able to return to university in Palermo I started to compete at regional events.

I'm still not sure how obvious my limp is to others today, but I certainly know the pain is still there. It would be easy to ask, "Why me?" and to complain about how unlucky I was that afternoon; nowadays I consider more fitting to ask, "Why not me?" considering my natural inclination for thrill-seeking activities. However, my experience has made me realise that I'm capable of doing much more than I ever imagined before my near death experience. Since then, I've enjoyed every moment of the roller-coaster ride life has had to offer. Ironically, the unforgettable date 9.4.94 became my signal for change, my brush with death has made me see life from a positive perspective that I wouldn't have had, if I'd carried on the road I was riding, literally! It's important to pay attention to the signs we are given.

Later in life I looked up the meaning of the numbers associated with my accident on the 9th April 1994, or 9494, which is a message to learn from the lessons in your life. My experience has taught me to feel more and to approach life more meaningfully and that what matters is not the absence of challenge or discomfort, but the way I deal with them. Above all its taught me about my personal responsibility in being the best person I can be with whatever life throws at me. I've always been curious about most things, but this experience gave me the focus to research people's basic needs and the "empathic tools" to design wellbeing environments.

The accident had turned my world upside down with a legacy of relentless pain in my hips radiating to my back and I've since managed to accumulate further injuries by pushing myself to play various sports. I use the pain to motivate my endurance, not as an excuse for any setbacks and rather than avoid challenges, use them to learn and grow. Above all, experiencing pain has become my most extrinsic motivator for personal healthy living and to influence healthy living in others.

At the beginning, my main way of coping with the pain was to take painkillers and anti-inflammatories, however approximately twenty years on from the accident and due to the regular use of them, I found myself with an ulcerated stomach. So, I had to find alternative ways of coping with the pain which sparked my interest in exploring holistic therapies. I gradually started Yoga and breathing classes and slowly but surely this alien language has become a part of me. I'm not sure how much the stress of the hectic world we live in influences my pain levels, but I'm certain that it causes bad habits, like sitting at the computer for several hours or long car journeys without regular stops, which all contribute to my back pain.

Since the regular practice of Hatha Yoga and conscious breathing, my quality of life has greatly improved, allowing me to further develop those natural abilities for introspection experienced during my childhood. Every morning I practice Yoga poses whilst following Master Yogis teachings and this appears to ease some of my aches and pains even if only for a few moments; the awareness of body, mind and emotions has become my internal foundation. The Yoga poses also enable an internal process of mindful awareness about the small scale of my existence in contrast to the immensity of life, which helps to deal with any external pressures throughout the day. This meditative practice has ultimately taught me that wellbeing is a birth-right which can't be acquired through medicine alone. I also need to work on my own balance through moderation and compromise, and it's doing wonders for my life.

The part I enjoy most about the continuous learning of Yoga is the process of freeing myself from the constant bombardment of more and more information. This allows me to dedicate attention to the details of my microcosm and how this can influence the world around us. Some Yoga poses may look particularly challenging and they certainly are if you want to achieve them in complete stillness like the Yogi masters, but it's the process of learning to focus on the essence of the pose that I find fascinating and applicable to any situation in personal and professional lives.

Yoga is about learning to be at peace with my own imperfection; when the Master says: *"Listen to your body first, then listen to me"* I use that awareness to improve my everyday capabilities. I practice Yoga most days of the week and my wife often tries to persuade me to take a break on days when I feel my pain levels are higher than usual; I then remind myself that if I stop training whenever my back hurts, I'd spend my most of my days on the sofa. Perhaps the outcome of my accident wasn't only an opportunity for a second chance but a way to deepen my resolve.

Amelia

Following my degree, I first travelled through other parts of Europe to experience the work of master architects that influenced my work. To name but a few I visited Renzo Piano's: Remodelling and Refurbishment of the Lingotto Industrial buildings; the Aquarium in the port of Genoa; the Church of Padre Pio in San Giovanni Rotondo in Italy; the National Centre of Science and Technology in Amsterdam and the Pompidou Centre in Paris. Whilst in Paris, I also experienced Jean Nouvelle's Arab World Institute and Dominique Perrault's National Library of France. In Spain and Portugal I experienced the work of minimalist architects such as Juan Navarro Baldeweg's Puerta Toledo Library in Madrid, Conference Centre in Salamanca, Alvaro Siza's Museum in Santiago de Compostela and during the World Exhibition in 1998 the Portuguese Pavilion in Lisbon. They're all architects that I've studied and admire for their continuous research for the essence of a design response to a context.

Upon return to my home town Pozzallo, Santo, a friend of mine who studied Architecture in Palermo at the same time as I did, told me about an opportunity to live and work abroad with a European grant, like the "Erasmus" program, called "Leonardo" for recent graduates.

Without pause for thought, I applied to work abroad and opted for work placements in England, Iceland or Spain. At school I'd mainly studied Latin and English, so I thought if I was accepted in any of the three countries, I'd enrol on a language course to learn the local language.

Madrid opened a window of opportunity, again thanks to Santo who introduced me to Almudena, an architect based there. Santo and I shared the rent for a studio apartment in La Latina and we started working with a group of architects including Spanish, Italian, German and English colleagues, on the international competition project "Europan 5" to build a new housing development which reflected the local mix of ethnicities in an area of Almeria, a port town on the Mediterranean Sea, originally founded by the Arabs on a Roman settlement.

The project for the area needed to consider the suburban connection with the town, the challenges of an eroding hill topography and dilapidated residential buildings in an urban settlement that reflected the social and financial problems of the ethnic mix living in the area. It was important to learn about the residents' culture, which was predominantly formed by a Gypsy community.

Returning to Madrid where our design group operated, I got to know some people from the Gypsy community, who introduced me to the culture within a culture that existed in La Latina. I was invited to gatherings not usually open to strangers and spent time in basements, accessible via narrow streets and alleyways, where the gypsies would congregate to play flamenco during the night; these gatherings weren't a show, it was their custom to get together to tell each other what had happened during the day through songs, with a few drinks.

Our group's project aimed to achieve the urban and architectural renewal of the area considering social, economic, and cultural regeneration, introducing a design for a new housing development that supported the residents' culture and was suitable for the climate and topography. From the first site visit, it was clear that the challenge of the steep differences in levels throughout the whole area, was a feature that needed to be enhanced because from many areas, it facilitated panoramic views over the Mediterranean Sea and rooftops. Our design was based on a concept of a residential unit with a small court, forming a microclimate with shade, a tree and a water feature as a respite from the heat. The units were grouped to form a bigger court supporting the congregation of families. The site was conceived like a landscaped park, rooted in the traditional English model of the Garden Village, housing helped to form a system of landscaped terraces; the system of lived-in retaining walls was strategically open at different levels to offer framed views and was connected by a web of paths and staircases leading to a civic centre which was the main congregation point for the rest of the town.

It was my first experience living away from Palermo and Sicily, and I really enjoyed working with this international group of people in the multicultural environment that Madrid offered; I realised how our backgrounds influence our perspectives and discussions. The words of one of the Master Architects

I studied most, Frank Lloyd Wright, resonated with me during this experience: "...freedom and opportunity to be yourself...At your best...you have good foliage and eventually blossoms, then you bear your fruit."

We classified as finalists with publication of our work and the experience fuelled my appetite for design competitions, which I am still eager to take part in, sometimes successfully and sometimes not; what I love is the research process and the learning that comes from it, more than the result. I find that on the occasions where I fall short of top results, this provides me with a greater opportunity for growth than if I'd won the competition. What matters to me is not searching for perfection; this is difficult to achieve because a design response will always be a subjective interpretation through the eyes and the experience of the architect. Likewise, the design assessment is influenced by the subjective experience of its judging panel. What I like is the opportunity the competition work offers to try and improve my ability to respond to a specific design challenge.

The road to success (however this is measured) isn't easy or everyone would be great at what they do. However if we push ourselves outside of our comfort zones, life offers us endless opportunities to develop resilience and become better prepared to face challenges. Empathy towards yourself and others is a good place to start, and meditative practice can be a very healthy way to develop it. Learning to leap into the unknown and face any challenge, give it our best shot, and learn the resulting lesson independently from the result is an amazing journey. My love for design and improving peoples' lives has motivated me through the most uncertain periods with a can-do attitude.

Towards the end of my time in Madrid, in one of Jes's house parties, (a friend taking part in the competition work), I met a gorgeous and brilliant girl with a musical accent which sounded as foreign as mine, in a land that was obviously neither hers nor mine, I instantly liked her whatever her nationality. Amelia was from England and was working in Madrid as an English teacher for business.

We met on another couple of occasions before I had to leave Madrid and at first I couldn't tell whether she liked me or not. So, with approximately one week left before my flight, the last time I met her, I knew that time was running out and I needed to force fate, so I dared to kiss her whilst we were casually talking, catching her by surprise. What I feared may have resulted in a smack, transformed into eight days of being inseparable. I was in love with her!

The following day I invited her for a burger at McDonald's, (she still jokingly holds it against me), not great I know, but I wasn't interested in the food, I just wanted to understand her feelings towards me without the need to make an impression with an expensive restaurant. I then discovered that just as I'd asked about her to our friends in common after our first encounter, so had she. We spent the following year and a half in a long-distance relationship, during which every attempt to start living together was faced with obstacles for one reason or another, until we decided that we couldn't carry on in this way. Amelia was mine at last!

At first, since I was

involved in the family business, she came to live in Sicily for a year, at the end of which we decided to move to England. She's a vivid living presence and a never-ending source of joy and inspiration. It's difficult to find the right words to express her loving attention, influence, and support every day in my life. Amelia and I have been together since that chance kiss, creating a family of our own with our two teenage daughters, Roberta and Gabriella. We've also learnt to become a productive working team for the development of our architectural practice focusing on a partnership within the universe's duality of complementary energies, sharing and selfless contributions. She uplifts my heart and strengthens my spirit when the going gets tough just as much as when the going is good.

I've learnt a lot from Amelia as she effortlessly embodies the concepts of empathy and love. I'd had other relationships before meeting her, some too short to remember and others longer, which after a while, I found unfulfilling for one reason or another; perhaps I just wasn't ready to commit. The story between Amelia and I couldn't be any more different; we didn't come from the same country, we couldn't speak one another's language and we knew very little about each other's culture. Yet we understood each other instantly and spent time learning one another's language without getting bored, both remaining fully engaged in what we were trying to say.

We got married after the first four years living together, even if it felt like we'd been married since we first started living together. We still retain the same grit and determination to understand one another with undivided attention, even though we now speak both English and Italian fluently and the spoken language of the house is more akin to Esperanto. She's the most selfless person from whom I learn the meaning of love every day. We are complete opposites in everything we think or do, with a completely different approach to risk. If I instinctively say black in response to a question or situation, she would say white and vice versa. I don't think that there is anyone who knows me more intimately and challenges me more profoundly to make the right decisions, as well as supporting my quest for a project perfect fit and personal growth. We both believe love begins at home and hope to continue to be a good example to our girls by working on our differences in our everyday lives, certain in the knowledge of the tangible attraction between two opposites.

As someone who is easily distracted by my work and design explored in my thoughts, love has been a difficult feeling for me to receive, until recently. Whilst I find it natural to shower Amelia and my daughters with expressions of love, when I'm on the receiving end of affection, I typically make a joke or pull away. Amelia has always been able to see through this, giving me space to learn how to receive it.

I'd be lying if I painted a picture of pure harmony in our marriage at all times. Life offers us endless opportunities to express the differences in our ways of thinking, but our love has matured to a point where we try and understand one another's reasons and emotions, knowing that we work best together when we look after one another's interests, with the same discipline we put into our personal growth.

I come from a family which considers "actions speak louder than words" and love was expressed by what my parents provided for me and my siblings, not necessarily by saying "I love you". Reflecting on those early memories I've learnt that to love and to feel loved is a primary human emotional need, also for me and in doing so I've become more accepting than in the past, recognising that relationships bring a far deeper meaning to our lives than any accomplishments.

Amelia and I agree that long-lasting emotional love is a choice which we need to exercise daily to develop our own language. She is happy to share a fair proportion of her travels with me experiencing and taking photos of buildings she doesn't know anything about. This is her way of spending quality time with me, just as I watch shows and concerts she likes, not to mention clothes shopping! I admit that I'm easily distracted by work, either by need or simply because I like it, so if she wants me to do anything for her, I find it helpful to have a list so that I don't forget. Coming from a Mediterranean culture I've always valued the importance of physical touch, which I feel has brought us together since the first day, perhaps because it also satisfied one of Amelia's emotional needs. Our two daughters are our precious gifts and witness all of the above in action every day. They've both learnt to accept the competing areas of our lives, family life and the running of the family business, when sometimes the architect absorbs the father and husband in me.

During the year that Amelia and I lived in Sicily, one of my last work-related activities was to assist Professor Pietro Manno in the delivery of his architectural design course. Pietro was my Professor of Architectural Design who I had worked with for my thesis. During this time, I shared the experience I'd gained in my travels and coached a group of talented students with their selected projects in sites around Palermo, whilst continuing my collaboration and learning alongside Pietro.

The sites always presented a different set of issues associated to their contexts with design solutions which were not seeking technical perfection, rather the development of a decision-making process. I found that the different perspectives of the learning environments I'd left not long before were a great way to develop teamwork and relive the infectious enthusiasm and passion that drives most students in the run up to critical exams. I'm sure that I learnt just as much from the students as they learnt from me.

My time at university in this role was a regular exercise in creative design over multiple sites presenting different sets of influences. It was a way for me to balance what I was experiencing in practice with the students' fresh ideas and perspective as well as their curiosity for what life after graduation was like. It was probably the most inspiring academic experience of my life. However after one year I felt I needed to concentrate on my experience in practice. I liked the vibrant creativity of the design process free from regulatory constraints, but I was longing to see my projects built and tested with practical and technical solutions which were not destined to remain just on paper.

A stranger in a foreign land

After experiencing life in Spain and Italy we moved to the UK in 2001. When I first arrived in England my spoken and written English was extremely poor. Until then I'd used a mixture of broken English, Spanish and Italian to communicate with Amelia, but I soon discovered that the English I was taught at school sounded very different depending on where I was in the United Kingdom. Nevertheless I attended professional interviews in Glasgow, Bristol, Luton, Peterborough, Birmingham, Leeds, Sheffield and Hull with the determination that, if I was offered an opportunity, I could demonstrate what I had learnt in my travels and put it to good use whilst learning more of the local language.

What helped me was my ability to quickly sketch and visualise what I understood of buildings or details discussed, expressing myself with pen lines more than words.

David was the first partner to offer me a job in Hull and years later he affectionately told me that my English was atrocious, but it was fascinating how quickly I could synthesise what we had tried to discuss at the interview using extemporaneous sketches. I liked David from the start as I felt he took design as seriously as I did. Whilst working with him I learnt more about the culture of accuracy and quality required on projects to make the most creative designs stand the test of time. We would often travel to site visits, and he always had a humble and peaceful way about him and was never short of irony to deal with the head strong arrogance of my youth in our discussions. He always commented on my work without imposing any views, more like guiding me where to focus my attention, giving me space to understand what to amend, if necessary. Over the years I consistently felt he understood me. As a mentor he helped me to figure out what was important to resolve rather than telling me what to change and to this day we remain good friends.

I've always felt that sketching is my way of visualising what others may not see, to give intuitive clarity to potentially complex technical solutions, particularly when they accompany the engagement with project stakeholders who may not have similar technical backgrounds or familiarity with drawings. This has always been my way of remaining present in a state of creative flow while visualising how to shape the environment.

When I started working in England, I had to take a backward step careerwise, even though at that stage I'd already completed nearly five years of experience as a qualified architect in Italy and several years of apprenticeship shadowing my father's work.

My complete lack of experience in England didn't make me any less ambitious though. During my interview with David, I noticed that on the conference room walls, there was a display of all the Partner Architects' portraits who had worked at the practice since 1875, when it was first founded. I can still remember wishing to see my photo amongst those portraits. Since beginning as an Architectural Assistant in 2001, I progressed to become an Equity Partner in less than ten years.

I was eager to learn fast, so I approached the restart of my career in a foreign country with the enthusiasm of a child learning new experiences. Most of the people I've met since moving to the United Kingdom have been very welcoming and given me the opportunity to demonstrate how I can add value. However as clients' attention and appreciation for my work began to increase, I also started to experience less appreciative comments from work colleagues usually aimed at me being a foreigner or my broken English. I wouldn't necessarily label this as a form of racism, but an obvious weakness that some people liked to point out, as if nobody had already noticed. I remember, while working for one of the Practices, having achieved UK recognised qualifications as Architect and CDM Principal Designer in the first five years living in the country, I asked if I could have support towards achieving a Project Management qualification. The response wasn't what I had expected. Instead, my Manager suggested I attend elocution lessons to lose my Italian accent. My Italian accent is still as strong as it was when I first arrived, however I've learnt to redirect my frustrations about those times to forge my own path of empowerment.

I didn't have anyone around me with similar experiences to learn from, and I wasn't always able to hide my frustrations from Amelia. My respite was again to turn to my design work, daydreaming of transformative, positive environments. In any career there are inevitable ups and downs, and I learnt from whatever came along the way.

By the time I arrived to the UK my early architectural experience had mainly been focused on residential developments and the education sector. However, just before arriving I'd completed the design of a day centre for people with learning disabilities on the ground floor of a school originally designed by my father a few years before, in my native town in Sicily. I'm not sure if it was a coincidence, but the experience of designing for special needs proved to be very useful for my first project, which was a Medium Secure Unit at this practice.

I didn't have any experience of working in mental health environments, so it was a different dimension from the residential projects I'd previously completed. The one-off housing was always exciting but the perception of patients' improvement in a well-designed, mental health environment was much greater. It was the opening to continuous research on what was most effective for the design of such environments, listening to feedback from the clinical team and occasionally what the residents themselves were happy to share.

From 2001 until the end of 2013, I built my career mainly in the same Practice (four years at Practice A in Hull, 18 months at Practice B and 18 months at Practice C in Darlington and seven years back in Hull at Practice A). East Yorkshire and particularly Hull has that "go 'n get it" spirit of the fishermen I was familiar with from my hometown. As soon as I drove into the area for the first time, although the colours of the sea were different and the icy salt air split my bare hands, I saw the Humber Bridge opening the door towards the North Sea and felt that Hull was a city where I could develop. I used to live and work in the memorable High Street in the old town and found most people welcoming and eager to show me the culture of the area and embrace me as one of their own. Some people were less welcoming and more inclined to denigrate Hull's history, perhaps wanting to protect the unassuming qualities of the place from the attention of outsiders. I've heard it many times: "Why would anyone from

Alessandro Caruso

Italy want to live here?" and at the time I didn't known how to take it. Such humility is a great contrast to the groundbreaking entrepreneurial spirit of so many other people. The blend of the many aspects of Hull is masterfully described by Philip Larkin in the poem "Here" which offers profound verses that have helped me to develop my sense of belonging to the place with ever deeper reflections.

Here

Swerving east, from rich industrial shadows
And traffic all night north; swerving through fields
Too thin and thistled to be called meadows,
And now and then a harsh-named halt, that shields
Workmen at dawn; swerving to solitude
Of skies and scarecrows, haystacks, hares and pheasants,
And the widening river's slow presence,
The piled gold clouds, the shining gull-marked mud,

Gathers to the surprise of a large town:
Here domes and statues, spires and cranes cluster
Beside grain-scattered streets, barge-crowded water,
And residents from raw estates, brought down
The dead straight miles by stealing flat-faced trolleys,

Push through plate-glass swing doors to their desires—
Cheap suits, red kitchen-ware, sharp shoes, iced lollies,
Electric mixers, toasters, washers, driers—

A cut-price crowd, urban yet simple, dwelling
Where only salesmen and relations come
Within a terminate and fishy-smelling
Pastoral of ships up streets, the slave museum,
Tattoo-shops, consulates, grim head-scarfed wives;
And out beyond its mortgaged half-build edges
Fast-shadowed wheat-fields, running high as hedges,
Isolate villages where removed lives

Loneliness clarifies. Here silence stands
Like heat. Here leaves unnoticed thicken,
Hidden weeds flower, neglected waters quicken,
Luminously-peopled air ascends;
And past the poppies bluish neutral distance
Ends the land suddenly beyond a beach
Of shapes and shingles. Here is unfettered existence:
Facing the sun, untalkative, out of reach.

I'm very grateful for the opportunities and experience matured whilst working at all three firms, however ultimately, I didn't feel any of them provided me with the space to cultivate the individuality of my work. The systems were often inherited and appeared to be applied just because someone had put them in place for whatever reason; the conversations amongst partners appeared to focus mostly on the commercial aspects of running the Practice, without time for discussions about the quality of work produced and the assignment of projects appeared to be based mostly on a hierarchical reasoning which didn't fit my free-spirited nature.

I've never believed that I'm truly employable and throughout my senior management positions, I also became concerned about who I'd become in the long run in an environment that I didn't feel was mine, much more than how much I was earning financially.

It became obvious to me that the anguish of staying in a situation where I wasn't happy was stronger than the thought of change. Since my accident I'd learnt to work on my resilience and positive thinking and from the experience of working for other practices I realised that I should focus my efforts on setting up my own practice. The words of the Dalai Lama resonated with me: *"sometimes not getting what you want is a wonderful stroke of luck"*.

The decision to take the risk of leaving a steady income that had provided a comfortable lifestyle for me and my family, to having none, wasn't an easy one. In the run up to making the decision I suffered many stressful and sleepless nights, but I could see the growth opportunity that would come out of it. This wasn't something that I'd shared with Amelia or anyone else in the family. I knew I had to trust my instincts and rely on my talent and resourcefulness before asking for any opinions. Having a young family, the risks were countless, yet I felt that it was a decision I needed to take without external influences to be sure of my deep resolve to succeed.

I remember calling Amelia after my last Partners' meeting in December 2013 to say that I'd confirmed my decision to retire from the practice. Amelia was in shock; we had a holiday to America coming up, which I asked her to cancel as soon as possible, along with any luxury expenditure. We needed to be ready for a period of no income.

With the bank demanding repayment of the loan I'd borrowed to buy my shares in the practice, I called my father to say that I'd left the Practice to set up my own, he was even more shocked than Amelia and he didn't hide his disapproval about my decision, expressing a number of real concerns. He thought that I'd worked so hard to become an equity partner in an architectural practice in a foreign land, that it was mad to risk it all without any certainty of success. He confirmed that he wouldn't be able help me financially. The tone of the call made me feel that I'd taken a disastrous decision, however he gently ended the conversation by saying that as he'd been able to do it years before, so could I.

If I initially took my father's words as rejection, soon enough they strengthened my focus and determination to satisfy my ambition to set up my own practice. Having had the experience of buying shares in my previous practice at the start of the recession in 2008, I'd already proved to myself that I wasn't afraid of taking risks. Our practice has now survived the financial shocks of new recessions, a Brexit process, a pandemic and in those moments, I still re-live the moments when it all began. After all, it may have been riskier to have played it safe and remain where I was.

I knew my father was right in his concerns and without a doubt his words made me reflect on the power of those moments to exercise my choice for a fight, flight or freeze response. When I'd previously left each of the Practices I'd worked for, I knew that they didn't provide a supportive environment for what I wanted to achieve. This time, I didn't want to wait any longer to work on my dream and vision, so I needed to trust my instincts and fight. Nevertheless, I was conscious that the probability of success for any business in the first three years is extremely low, yet I could see the learning opportunity. I felt my heart was in the right place and confident that I could hold my nerve and rely on my strengths to get the practice up and running.

My beginner's mind was put to the test once again. It was very different compared to when I first arrived in England, and I can't hide that it was rather difficult to keep a positive and enthusiastic beginner's mindset when you know people are watching you, wondering if you will succeed. The words of Abraham Lincoln kept returning to my mind: *"it's not the years in your life, it's the life in your years"*.

Amelia and I used all our life savings and my mother and Amelia's parents offered to help with a loan, which we borrowed as an emergency fund, should circumstances take a turn for the worse. Luckily, we managed to pay them back within the first two years.

I was ready to take the responsibility for my decision and not to expect that the people who knew me would understand my pursuit for creating a more fulfilling environment where to grow personally and professionally.

Regrettably the process of retiring my capital investment in the business took an adversarial and acrimonious turn almost as soon as I stepped out of the practice building, so I spent most of the run up to the Christmas holidays resolving legalities with my accountant and solicitor. The anger and frustration experienced during my retirement process, was offset by my daydreaming and writing my first business plan which I used to speak to banks and agree the terms of repayment of my old loan.

Soon enough, early in January 2014 my architectural practice was born with Amelia's help, working from our dining room table like most people who have started similar journeys. Technology provided a helping hand in the form of a laptop and software I knew how to

operate. There I was at the centre of it,
having rejected a senior position in one of the oldest
architectural practices in the United Kingdom
at the time, with all the benefits that went
with it, yet happy to find my freedom in the
direction of my design and my unconventional
approach to an architect office.
I was conscious of all limitations, however I felt
that having less money was another
opportunity to work on my creative skills to
make things happen; a similar skill to what I use
during any value engineering exercises to ensure
our projects are delivered on time, on budget
and to the agreed quality standards.

I like searching for questions in my readings.
One I often reflect on is the one
a Zen master asked his disciples:

*how do you step forward from the
top of a one-hundred-foot pole?*

On this occasion, for me the answer was a leap into the
unknown and the beginning of an extraordinary journey.

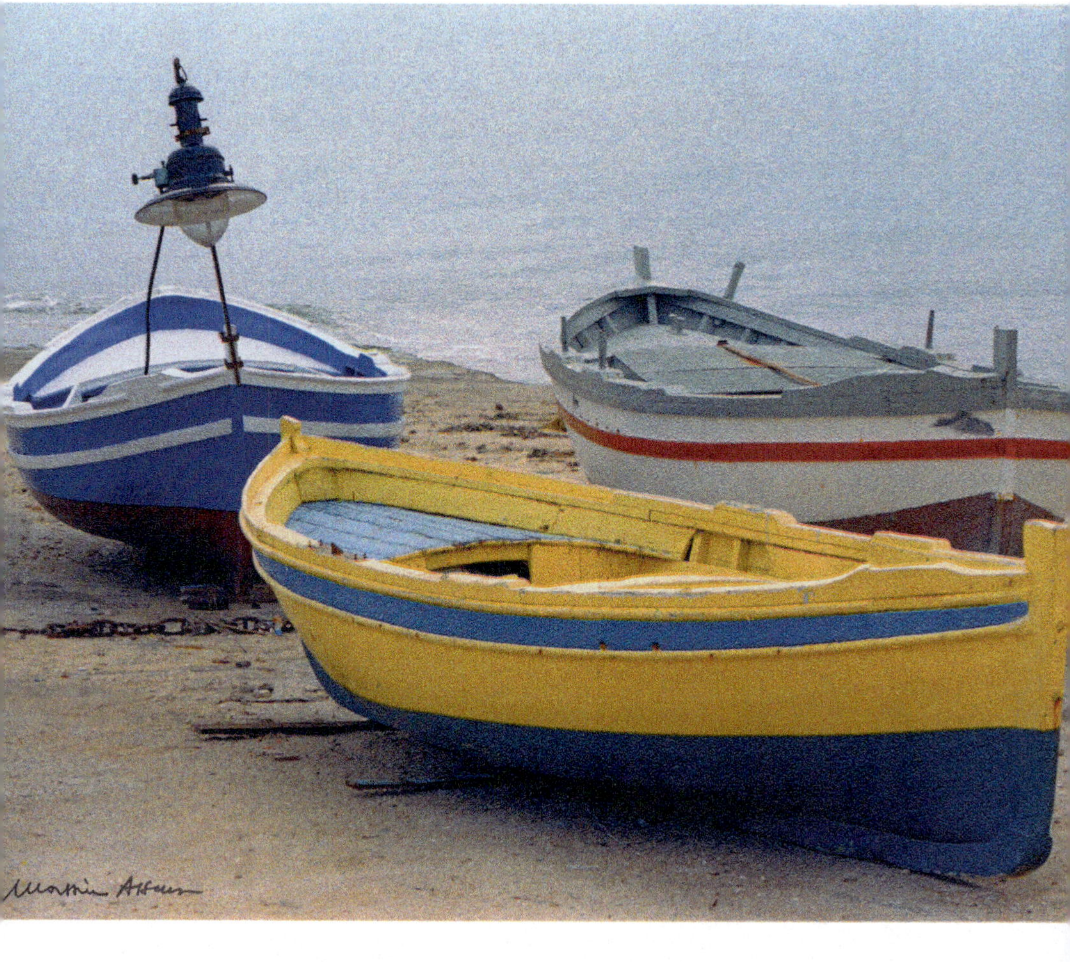

Your turn...
How does your background influence your mission?

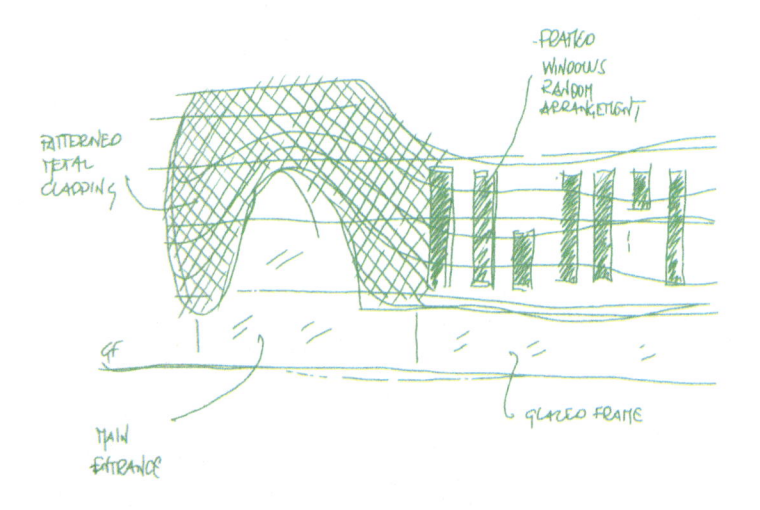

Festina Lente
(Hurry Slowly)

"Arriving at each new city, the traveller finds again a past of his that he did not know he had: the foreignness of what you no longer are or no longer possess lies in wait for you in foreign, unpossessed places."

Invisible Cities, Italo Calvino

In February 1999, following a fantastic few days with Amelia at Lake Bracciano near Rome, on the drive back, I gave a lift to a Buddhist Zen monk I'd met in a service station. We immediately felt at ease with one another, speaking about anything which made my journey back to Sicily more interesting and above all enlightening. He told me a story, which made a huge impression on me, about the role of a chef in a monastery and the chef's way of practicing his skills. Just before I dropped him off, he concluded the story by telling me that the duty of a Zen chef is to prepare the best and most succulent meal with the ingredients available, even if they're only water and rice. There's no point in complaining about the ingredients that aren't available.

I wake up every morning around half past five and start my day with some training, Yoga and meditation: it's my way of creating a place for my mental, emotional, physical, and spiritual wellbeing. I use my meditative practice to slow my pace down and become more receptive to learn how to perform my roles in life with authenticity and simplicity, and, following the Zen chef's principle, to craft my designs with what life has to offer. It doesn't matter how much I have of what's available, it's all I need; the difference is how I make use of it.

My accident opened my eyes on the difference between physical and emotional pain. When I started my recovery, I became more sensitive to it and realised that pain was all around me. Where people saw anguish and despair, I started to feel an emotional bond with the people that were experiencing pain or some form of recovery from it; I could also see how the design of the environment could make a difference.

No matter how much people have in life, pain can touch us in different forms. Having experienced pain directly, I promised myself to dedicate my life to injecting empathy into my designs to create the best environments I can for all of us with whatever life has to offer me. Such intentionality doesn't have any limitations of time, space or magnitude: it became a determination, more than a belief, that even if my designs positively impact the life of just one person, I've made a meaningful contribution to their happiness, relying only on my imagination.

I founded Alessandro Caruso Architecture & Interiors Ltd (ACA) with Amelia's help without any projects in sight, but with a compelling vision that I was raring to put into place. I wanted to create a Practice with a balance between commercial aspects and social values, so my meditation would focus on principles learnt along the way on how to live and design a more fulfilling life, based on five main elements. Firstly, ACA's work should be based on building long-term relationships with everyone, be it colleagues, consultants, contractors, or clients. Secondly, it would also need to provide a living whilst allowing me to learn about myself and how to become a better designer to help others. Thirdly, I wanted ACA to be socially involved in the community. Fourthly, I wanted to help people and transform their lives. Finally, I wanted to focus on designs that nurtures a more harmonious relationship with our planet.

The reason I delved deeper into spirituality was to slow down and keep a balanced perspective on life that would allow me to ponder about what I wanted to achieve for myself and for others.

With the blank slate of setting up ACA, I couldn't wait to devote my life to what I loved. In the process I hoped to inspire others by offering employment and professional development to students. Researching how to become an instrument of change to make a positive impact on people had become my personal drive. My vision was ambitious: to offer an immersive experience for everyone, creating an innovative environment designed through collaboration. I've always been aware that I can't achieve this on my own, therefore I dedicate my time to developing all round apprentices who will hopefully one day pass onto others what they learn from me.

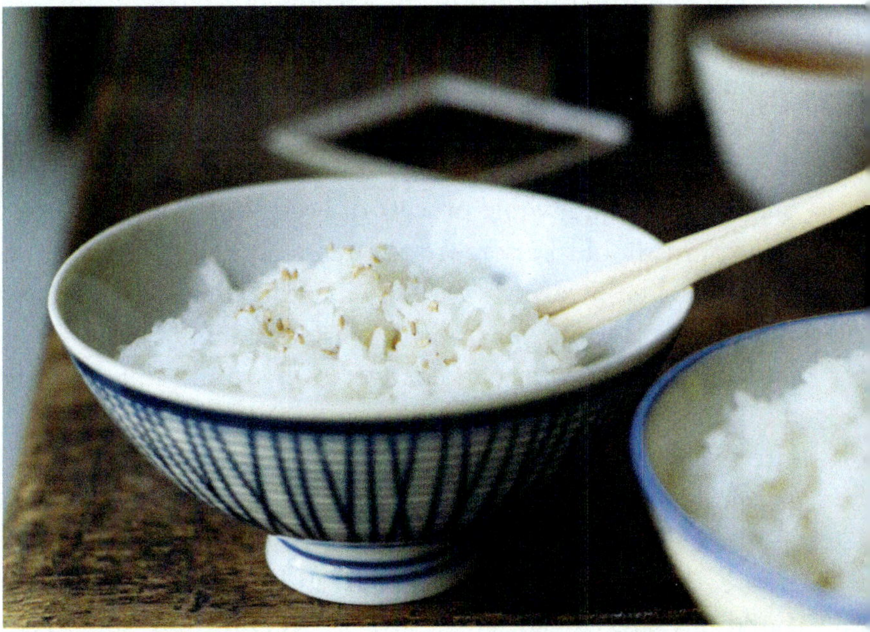

Change

Throughout my work experience in other practices, I'd noted almost a disconnect between the concept design team and the technical design team. I've always loved the transformative process which begins as a concept and becomes a completed building. I fundamentally believe that if you know how to build you know what to build and if you know what to build you know how to build it. It's one of the catch twenty two situations of this profession and I've therefore focused my career on ensuring that my concept design skills are on a par with my technical skills. I still find it difficult to delegate parts of a project to others, which I recognise is a stubborn limitation, yet I can't help being curious about the discovery journey that a project can offer at any stage. I enjoy the whole process of every new project on our drawing boards, or should I say more accurately, developed on our computers. Likewise, I enjoy every day of my life; each day is unique, and I like to pay attention to the meaning of what I'm doing.

In life everything is energy in a continuous transformation. Buildings' components are a combination of basic elements such as fire, water, metals, earth and air. Such a combination process is a magical, alchemic process that requires a great deal of time and faith to see how the concept vision will transform into a building. I like to be aware of every aspect, where to add details, where not to, how buildings are constructed, always listening to everyone involved without my ego getting in the way.

This process is very similar to the awareness of our emotions. Anger or frustration for example, can be negative emotions if driven by our ego. However, without our ego they can be positive emotions, such as determination. Likewise, greed can be positive if driven by a willingness to help others rather than just yourself.

Through my contemplative practice, I've become more aware that life provides all the elements we need to bring our greatest ideas to fruition: matter, light, sound, colours, textures, food and flower essences. Such elements can all be used to find harmony in a building to make it look heavy or light, transparent or solid, monochromatic or colourful and tactile or smooth. They're equally important and form a critical part of ACA's building design.

Different architects may use these basic elements in different ways that may be more conservative or provocative. I prefer to take some risk, often without fear of failure; to offer a different perspective from the initial brief that perhaps hadn't been considered: risk can sometimes be a positive agent of change. I love that moment before the initial ideas are shared with the client, where I hope to have correctly interpreted the brief and that the project will evolve in the way I expect it to. Yet I also welcome that opportunity, when client feedback may present a perspective which none of us had considered previously, which would result in a wider ownership of the final design.

Clearing and awareness

Every new project is exciting and forges new relationships regardless of the sector; commercial, education, residential or healthcare. My team and I become eager to start visualising design ideas, while still working on other projects. However, it's difficult to see which sensory elements the project brief offers us, without clearing our desks from other distractions. Then, we read the context of the new project and discuss possible themes to develop. On the surface, some new projects appear very similar to others previously completed, yet we always start afresh. A review of lessons learnt from previous projects offers us the opportunity to see where we can make a start.

I've always started my day very early. When I first arrived to the UK, I used this time to study for new qualifications. As my roles changed, instead, I started the working day by reading documents or making calls. Since setting up ACA, I like to start my day meditating; even on days I have to set off early to travel to sites, it's my only opportunity to clear my mind in readiness for the day ahead. To meditate, I don't have a dedicated space or use objects as inspiration, simply a dedicated time in the early morning before family life starts. In the silence of my meditation, the awareness of thoughts and feelings that influence my everyday life soften their intensity, like the waves caused by the wind on a lake: when the surface of the lake is finally smooth, I can see the image reflected on it from a detached perspective that helps me to see things more clearly.

When I first arrived in England, I was conscious of the difficulties of a re-start in my early thirties, yet I believed in what Eckart Tolle stated: *"being at ease with not knowing is crucial for the answers to come to you"*. Similarly, my daily meditation helps me to re-start and create space for more, to see the possible energy balance of all elements of a project; it isn't a space that is void but a space that is full of possibilities like the clouds that form in a blue sky. At the heart of this space is my body and the relationships I build with people and the environment through my thoughts, emotions, and actions: sometimes I can use all the elements and ideas that I come into contact with, others in different proportions or some not at all; sometimes discarded ideas can influence parallel or future projects; it's therefore important for me to practice my awareness to expand the boundaries of my perspective.

I adopt the same approach with the apprentices that join the team. Rather than trying to make them fit a position I have in mind, Amelia and I spend time understanding their strengths, so they can flourish through the design process. In this case, meditative practice helps to free my mind from any conditioning of past experiences and to become aware that people can change from one day to the next. I find it's not only important to understand my conditioning but also other people's conditioning and to start every day afresh.

Don't get me wrong I don't think, neither do I promote the idea that my meditation helps me to remove any issues or problems needing my attention. On the contrary, it helps me to see them more clearly and how to resolve them. For me, meditation is an endless process. Life will always present challenges to be resolved on a personal or a project level. What I perceive to be the right thing to do is my only resource. Regardless of the challenge, what matters is that I can see clearly and take action.

The experiences I share with my team in the office becomes my daily opportunity to clarify my thoughts for my apprentices as much as for me. I'm also conscious that the same clearing my mind and the awareness of the meditative process will be required again tomorrow for a fresh start.

Enthusiasm of a child

Most people who know me will recognise my enthusiasm in starting a new project. Like a child, I can't wait to discover the infinite opportunities that may develop. I'm still fascinated with this way of learning, as no matter how much we know already, there is always an opportunity to learn more. Children wouldn't read a book on how to walk before trying to walk; they simply get up and start with the first step. After every fall, they try again until they succeed, despite any frustration or pain in the learning process. I'd say that I'm still in that stage of design development, with an innate stubbornness not to be set back by any adversity in the process.

It's through frustration and pain that we may be able to learn the most, particularly about ourselves. In life, we can easily avoid what we are afraid of, yet when we learn to face our fears, we can learn the most about ourselves.

ACA's projects help me to satisfy my deep-seated need to be on other people's teams, while inspiring and nurturing my own team. These projects are often a formal manifestation of what I understand about the brief through the lens of who I am; they become an opportunity for me to openly share my personal reflection on the content without judgement, uncovering the most critical elements required to create a supportive environment. My meditation is an important part of this learning process as it helps me to see clearly and without judgement, who I am and my changing role throughout the project. For example, I often recognise my limitations and expect a lot from my team as I do from myself. Such determination often pushes me to move quickly, running the risk of upsetting people with a more sensitive nature. It doesn't help that I am also single-minded when I have an end goal in sight. However, an advantage is that I'm determined, don't give up easily and am prepared to wait until the right moment for things to go in my direction; I like to think that ACA's work reflects such determination.

When we understand our characteristics well, they become our main ingredients for what we want to achieve in life. I don't believe that our characteristics can only be categorised as positive or negative. We may prefer some and not others. Different societies may value some more than others, therefore it's a subjective perspective. This is one of the reasons why I focus my meditation on trying to see things without judgement. I'm naturally inclined to being judgemental and having personal opinions, however I've learnt that it's a natural characteristic of being human. When I find myself being judgemental, I try to remind myself that I'm conditioned by that precise moment and may take a different view later on.

Through meditation, I've learnt to recognise the emotions I feel at any time. It could be jealousy, sadness, or happiness; I limit myself to recognise them and accept them as part of who I am in that moment and let them transition freely through my life. I try to do the same with what I recognise as my negative emotions, trying to understand how they work and whether they can be harnessed as a resource instead of letting them hold me back. This approach also helps me to understand others more deeply.

Since setting up in practice, Amelia and I have converted our garage, designed, and built our garden studio before moving into a commercial office as the team of apprentices grew. The majority have joined us as architecture or interior design students from a diversity of backgrounds. Amelia and I have always made the most of our differences to facilitate our growth and over the years we've enjoyed working with apprentices from Italy, Poland, Pakistan, India and the Middle East as well as the United Kingdom.

I believe that the diversity in our creative environment goes beyond the equality at work. There's a level of open-mindedness in embracing our different cultures and backgrounds which enhance our perspectives and abilities to see what others don't. Every day we work on the creative chemistry that unites us, mixing and matching the diverse elements that come from working with clients and other consultants to create something unique. ACA is a simple set up: I'm an architect at work with an interest in developing the careers of the apprentices who join, to learn and to help me with their skills and talents, throughout the life of a project. Following an initial conversation regarding a new project, around concepts and details with all manners of sketches, most are free to move the assigned project forward through all stages, with my guidance. I believe that we rise by lifting others, therefore as their experience with the practice grows, I invite them to inspire and share what they've learnt with newer members of the team to support a "give and take" role for all of us.

Amelia and I spend time, in car journeys and over coffee to get to know each one of our team members on a personal level, which is usually a great opportunity to learn about the thoughts and ideas of the quieter ones. Some have left ACA and have taken what they've learnt elsewhere, whereas the majority embrace and enjoy the freedom to learn on the job with great loyalty. A few of them are developing to be the best interpreters and developers of the pen sketches that come from my hand, granting me the freedom to research and explore more. They all help me to understand and resolve any issues associated to our project systems and procedures or practice administration. Although we seek continuous improvement, I'm under no illusion that problems will always arise and that not everything can be exactly as I want. However, in the process, we always improve our understanding and ability to collaboratively resolve any situations arising in our professional and personal lives.

On a personal level, I've come to realise the importance that doubt, faith and determination play in everything I do. Over the years, some people have considered my natural inclination to doubt before taking important decisions as a weakness, yet I consider this open-mindedness, which is a fundamental condition of spontaneity at the start of a new project or activity.

No matter how successful a project is, or what we've achieved and learnt along the way, I'm wary of remaining too attached to the sense of satisfaction, which may lead to complacency. I make a point of asking myself frequently "who am I?" as a husband, a father, a son and a brother in life, or simply as an architect in my profession, to understand the role I'm living in the moment. I also recognise the role that faith played when I decided to leave the benefits of a career in other professional practices and the determination required to set up my own practice.

"One day without work is a day without eating."

When I set up the Practice, I knew that I didn't want to always be shackled by commercial decisions, I knew that we don't live to work, yet I could see the importance of working with a purpose to live. I wanted ACA to embrace the words of Gandhi *"Right Thoughts, Right Words & Right Deeds Change the World"*. These words inspired a spiritual part of me that I generally prefer to keep private, that over the years has revealed to me the interdependence between my work, human beings and our planet. Therefore, a good day's work needed to produce enough to sustain my family; including those of the people we employ, allow us to put some funds away for growth and uncertainty and to serve the community and mother earth. I believe that we make a difference in people's lives by how we do our work. So, it was clear to me that ACA needed to be a vehicle of training for professional and personal growth for students in architecture and interior design. To achieve this, ACA needed to expand its presence and experience in fundamental sectors with a high social impact, such as healthcare and education, as well as to be recognised for design excellence. I use my meditative practice to reflect on how to craft a mindful experience that helps people to develop harmonious interpersonal relationships and with the environment.

At ACA, we work in teams with a focus on study, apprenticeship and supporting charitable activities. I've devoted myself to training, self-development and spiritual transformation; along with Amelia and members of the team that have joined us, we've been able to achieve great progress. As new members of the team join us, they develop the idea of interdependence, learning from colleagues that have been at ACA for longer. Each year, ACA supports one or more charities associated to our projects, either financially to raise funds for research or by volunteering.

Within my specialism, I've always known that it's not possible to know everything, I rather focus on retaining the open mind of a child and dedicating my time to further research and research-based charitable organisations and activities. Over the years, Amelia and I have invited mentors with relevant experience to advise us on how to improve our sector-specific services and growth, dedicating attention to every detail of our systems and processes.

Despite the speed at which the industry moves, I love to indulge in the details of our projects. I like the fact that I need to slow down during the design stage to fully consider them. Once the building is complete, I'd like to think that some people may also slow down to notice these details and appreciate that someone has taken the time to think about them; I believe such details are what makes a good project, because for instance, they can help the building-users to be selective in what they want to look at or to distract them from looking at what's not important.

Prior to coming to England, I'd benefited from the work experience in my family business. Was setting up a Practice in another country different? My pragmatic approach led me to focus on understanding the priorities and establishing the time-frames to achieve them, above all I focused on being mindful of doing one thing at a time.

This approach is not dissimilar to the one I use for many of our projects, we: understand our costs; estimate our yearly cash-flow; refine our understanding of which projects (and in further detail which stages) are most profitable and rewarding and the reasons behind; understand the best people and software to enhance our attention to detail and other resources required to pursue excellent results and ultimately sustain our growth.

To live a life, run an activity or a project, one must focus on the common denominator which is paying attention to the details. In the early days, I summarised every detail in a business plan that became a critical document to speak with family and banks to convince them that we had a clear understanding of our specialism, the market and how to penetrate it. With a spirit of gratitude, I managed to convince the bank that rather than declaring me bankrupt, because I was unable to repay the loan I'd taken out to buy the shares in my previous practice, I could commit to an extended arrangement to repay the existing loan. I also managed to gain trust from family members to agree to a loan that we could use as a war chest, if the period of no commissions lasted longer than envisaged, on the proviso that we would try not to touch it and repay it within two years. Meanwhile, we used all our life savings to get the Practice going, spending the bare minimum.

I can't describe the anxiety of seeing the bank account going down as I continued to make calls and travel around the country to seek project opportunities. After the first six months of next to no commissions despite potential ones, it was becoming a struggle to make a living from the Practice and self-doubt started to creep in. I started to consider accepting senior job appointments rather than seek new projects. I had a few interviews, but when it came to the question of what would happen to ACA, I couldn't deny my intention to keep it afloat alongside any employment. Regrettably, the employment offers were only valid with no strings attached, so I had to trust my instincts and carry on with plan A. So much sweat and blood had gone into establishing ACA, that I couldn't let it go to waste. By the time we only had enough funds in the bank to last another month, fortunately, things began to change. With fate on my side, a few feasibility projects began to trickle in, offering us a lifeline, just in time!

This was a period of steep personal and professional growth and as invoices started to be paid, Amelia and I could see our accounts becoming healthier to the point that, over time, we were able to settle all financial commitments taken, within the agreed terms. We realised that at the end of the day, there's always sufficient time and money if you really want to make something happen and people can be gracious with their help if they can see that your heart and determination are in the right place.

I believe that one of the secrets of our achievements so far has been our informal, yet authentic approach, which at times may have appeared amateur to the eyes of peer experts. Every project starts from scratch, with a focus on understanding the people and the conditions we need to improve to create a connection. I deliberately refrain from submitting many details of past projects because I want to focus on what will be different with the current project. Instead of selling a preconceived ready-made project, I apply previous experience to analyse lessons learnt and to visualise how things could work in a different context. I see every new project as the enabler of a new flow for the building-users at physical, energetic and emotional levels, while becoming a balanced and harmonious presence in its context. I can only describe the process like meditation, taking the time to appreciate the silence which helps me to slowly uncover the critical elements requiring attention. It's the stimulating start of creative fantasies and the exciting first step of a new design adventure, which I admit at first instance, is my personal reading or analysis of a context. This analysis gains objectivity with the contributions of the extended project team.

We all place an emphasis on some aspects and not on others, looking through the lenses of our experiences, the importance for me is in the collaborative understanding of which elements, local to a project, allow us to establish a relationship with the vernacular context and the community. The base elements we use in our lives and projects are ultimately the same as the ones that make all human beings: earth, water, fire, air and space. They're all interconnected and each one influences the other to become a product, with defined proportions, that can ultimately become a new building. I find it mesmerising how anything we design at ACA, regardless of the size of the project, has a great influence on the environment, families and their generations. This understanding empowers me to use the resources offered by mother earth as responsibly as possible.

Our clients have made ACA's achievements possible so far and their projects remain our daily focus. I've long been a believer that our strongest marketing strategy is to focus on delighting our clients and building strong relationships so that they'll return. As our number of clients and projects increase, we regularly request feedback on their experience working with us, to ensure that we achieve an award-worthy building and above all, a design that is crafted to truly meets their needs.

I like to think that we achieve this by focusing on the present, at any one time, until a project is complete, without dwelling on what has been done before or what will be done in the future. My work becomes a form of meditative practice that allows me to focus on the here and now. When I view my work in this light, I find it a source of energy and mental peace rather than another tiring day at the office.

Despite my Catholic background, I've never mentioned the following before writing this book, because I don't advocate any specific religious faiths, however I like to use my meditation to understand what constitutes basic, human, positive qualities applicable to my work: positive feelings, a sense of involvement, honesty, discipline and creativity, supported by a motivating purpose. I also believe that at the heart of wellbeing is a deep rapport with ourselves and the relationships with the places we live in and work at and the people in our families and communities. I summarised this with the message associated to our Practice logo: Design for wellbeing.

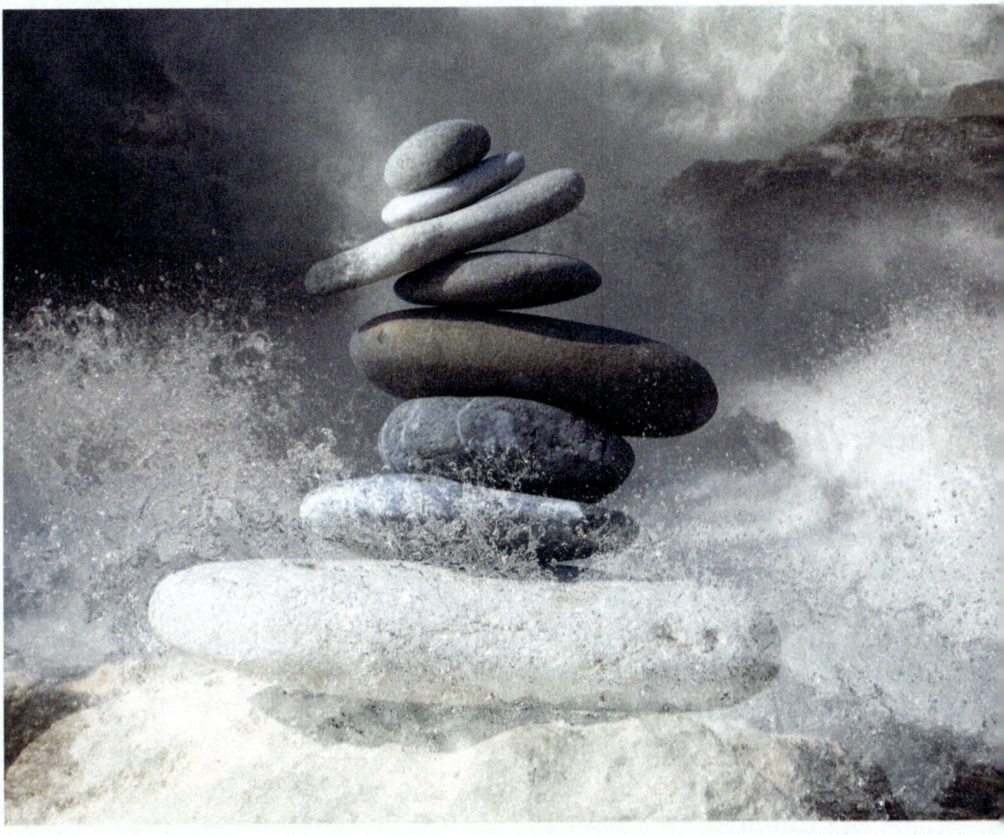

Who is our design for?

Having had firsthand experience of what it's like to be in a healthcare setting for quite some time, I've realised that the best way to improve these environments is to design them as if I were still there and see how the people around me would respond to the environment created. My role isn't limited to my eagerness to be involved in any project, fundamentally I like to investigate the conditions which generate wellbeing in people. To achieve this, I realised that I needed to start by understanding myself. It gradually became clear to me that if I could understand how to design for myself, I'd simultaneously be designing for everyone else. We're all connected and if we can harness our power of collaboration and cooperation nothing is impossible. The only way to move forward is to follow the human instinct of helping one another.

My interest in designing for others stems from my curiosity about what I can learn from the people I'm helping. While I try and understand people's contexts and conditions and look at the world through their eyes, I expand my vision of life and they become part of a collaborative design process; I see opportunities and inspiration for design as I learn what they require.

Every project becomes a design story told through the unique eyes of the people involved, including (in the case of healthcare projects) the patients' perspectives in helping them to revive their interest in the world and transform whatever despair into hope. Unlike the story of a book, the design story will last for the lifetime of the building, with endless twists and turns to understand people's emotional responses to an environment and how the design of physical surroundings can support positive emotions.

Over the last twenty years, I have closely followed the research of the Academy of Neuroscience for Architecture with parallel readings on the subject, to support my studies of the interface between architecture and neuroscience, it is a continuous discovery of how the world we perceive through our senses, triggers different areas of our brains to experience feelings such as awe, fear, peace or comfort.

I've already mentioned how the negative experience a badly-designed hospital environment had on my recovery. Therefore, I ponder, if people had to experience limited, crowded, poorly-lit and noisy environments all the time, and be isolated from friends and family, would such conditions burden their immune systems, in addition to their illnesses? Our physical surroundings can affect the way we feel and as a result can hinder the natural restoration of our body's balance; this ultimately affects our emotions and our speed of healing.

A critical part of my journey has been to understand how the brain becomes active. I've learnt what I can describe in simplistic terms that at a molecular level, when our senses are stimulated, blood flow in our brain increases, activating nerve cells which trigger electrical impulses and chemical processes that allow nerve cells to signal one another to recognise what we are perceiving.

In architectural terms it's important for me to understand how to stimulate the senses to provide comfort. When I was in my hospital room, I could see the rather distant and small window offering limited views. At the time, to comfort myself, I'd tell myself that I wouldn't be there long. Eventually I discovered the important effect that a view of nature has on healing and wellbeing: being able to see a variety of colours, light and movements of the natural habitat is calming and relaxing, without the need to be immersed in it. A window or simply an image on a wall or ceiling assumes a different significance when considered in those terms. It's important for me to design with an understanding of how light, colour and movement can affect the building-users' moods.

Seeing a different amount of sunlight can influence people's moods in an office or shopping environment and can have a significant impact on the length of stay in a hospital. The type of daylight can give a different perception of colour; it's also important to consider the history of our genes in perceiving colours. I found it fascinating to learn that the yellow-green range of colours was the first to be perceived in the history of human evolution, the blue range was part of our secondary evolution (around 500 million years ago) and the last to be perceived was the orange-red range around 30-40 million years ago. It explains how our eyes, having been accustomed to perceiving the colour green the longest, respond well to this relaxing colour, possibly creating an association to a primordial time in which we felt safe.

I like to use colours to define the orientation strategy of a building based on some of the studies I followed, particularly on dementia friendly design research. I understand that rooms with a blue hue are perceived to be calming, while using red or yellow hues are perceived as stimulating. For example, people have been reported to feel hungry or thirsty in orange rooms and energetic in yellow rooms; the use of colour hues can become a subtle strategy to influence people's behaviour, particularly in challenging healing environments.

When I was in my hospital bed I could hear the buzzing of the medical machinery in the room, nurse call alarms, footsteps on the hard-tiled floor, phones ringing and people's voices reverberating off walls and ceilings at a time when I was craving some silence to recover. I tried to distract myself by listening to music through my headphones, to try to uplift my emotions, but the external noise was just too loud and constant. When we listen to music, like with other senses, different areas of our brain are flooded with blood, leading to chemical processes releasing dopamine (associated to desire) or endorphins (the body's natural opioid) which depending on the type of music, influence our emotions. Like the view of a natural scene, some types of music can be calming, this is often echoing patterns of sounds like what we find in nature, such as the rain falling or waves crashing in the sea. When possible, I like to integrate some background relaxing music as part of a holistic acoustic strategy that focuses on minimising loud and startling sounds in any environment.

Also, through the sense of touch and smell we can relive emotions associated to our earliest childhood memories, as we come in direct contact with the physical environment. Through the sense of touch, we can form an image of an object because it relates to our sense of sight.

Our sense of smell is extremely sensitive and capable of identifying chemical particles based on the few molecules dissolved in the air and can help us inform a view of the physical environment and also perceive the mood of those around us, beyond the range of our eyes and ears.

Understanding how we gather information about the physical surroundings through all our senses and how hormones are released during emotional experiences is the embodiment of a person-centred design. This offers a fantastic source of influence to find new solutions that are adaptable to people's perception abilities as we all perceive our environments differently. Our challenges are to design physical environments which cater for endless evolutions of human beings and also to design in flexibility for potential, future adaptions to different uses.

Why am I doing this?

I believe that the intensity of my accident and the chain of reactions, from seeing the car in front of me up to my intuitive approach to recovery, created an opportunity for me to investigate those events, to find critical principles of design. Such design principles are at the intersection between technical and psychological aspects to help people and improve our communities. My investigation has become an endless mastering of a listening process, with a spirit of openness, that becomes an analysis of specific human conditions and illnesses, to understand how to generate empathic design solutions. How can I create a supportive physical environment that can trigger positive emotions, similar to those I seek in my meditative practice such as love and compassion, while reducing stress and anxiety? How can I support a healing process which isn't necessarily connected to the benefits of medicine? How does form follow the function while stimulating the senses, finding patterns, variations, techniques, and design ideas of a resilient physical environment that aims to respond to specific psychological situations? I hope my findings will become clearer as the book evolves.

From the early days of ACA's setup, we've embraced the use of technology to develop the designs of my early sketches, to visualise and communicate them plainly, using a Virtual Reality software. My talented colleagues grasp the use of such software almost intuitively, allowing me to stay focused on the ideas behind the concepts and the holistic design development of the environment.

The slow pace of the listening process, condensed into a few early sketches, leaves ample scope for my team to use their imagination and is counterbalanced by the fast pace of the design development, when each detail is connected to the next. The speed at which we convert ideas into a visualisation is key to moving the project towards reality. The visualisation becomes an early prototype of our projects, which are sufficiently developed to convey a variety of emotions to the viewer: the immersion in the virtual reality allows our clients to experience a blend of virtual comfort and excitement of being in their future building. It also allows the team to uncover any flaws in the design or to investigate further how to treat volume, space or details required. We deliberately share only a "sufficiently finished" project visualisation with clients, to allow for their design input in our collaborative approach for the following stages.

It's always a risk to let the client see my enthusiasm for their project when I reveal it in 3D, when the design is still not completely polished, as they may feel that the design has been finalised and can't be changed, for fear of hurting my feelings. On the contrary, it's a magical process where the sharing of thoughts allows communication to deepen into the materiality of the project. The virtual environment, from the early stages of the design process, helps the viewer to "live" the project. It generates an emotional and bodily response, that makes them part of the story, using their vision and hearing, which are the most important senses of orientation. It's also a way to test an authentic virtual relationship with the environment, where the viewer has a degree of control over the way they navigate around the building, using visual cues, supporting their desires for the finished building. Due to our work within mental health and dementia environments, at this stage we try to understand the role of the visual cues we want to introduce; they need to be memorable and evoke positive associations and be big enough to be seen from a distance.

Similarly, working on my spiritual and personal growth, in many respects, has allowed me to forget about the focus I had on myself before the accident, which has expanded my view of life. Who I am becomes less relevant as my understanding of the rest of the universe expands, allowing me to expand with it, without solution of continuity: there is no separation.

A nurturing environment

Having realised the importance of looking after myself through my Yoga and meditation, I wanted to create a caring, informal and familial environment based on open communication, collaboration and a flat hierarchy, which is focused on helping other people. Setting up ACA has enabled me to work on the creation of what I consider to be a nurturing environment. My focus is to identify myself with the team and become an agent of a collaborative learning experience, to uncover what they need to help me generate an emotional response with our designs. That is how we work and how every one of our projects starts, supporting the apprentices working with us to learn what is necessary for each stage of the project, without being under constant pressure. We've recently introduced an early finish on a Friday to have a longer rest over the weekend to help maintain a healthy workforce that can support us with fresh creativity and problem-solving skills. In my case, this strengthens my emotional intelligence to be able to bring out the best in the people I work with.

With the size of ACA in continuous evolution, I've not yet managed to design an office space that fully satisfies my aspirations for the expanding team. As we've grown and invited more apprentices to join us, we've temporarily moved to different environments, putting our own stamp on them, with screens showing our projects and the ACA logo.

As soon as we'd repaid all the loans, Amelia and I decided that, moving forward, we'd limit any borrowing in favour of pursuing a culture of reinvesting profits and applying for any applicable grants or funding available. Some of our equipment and software is still financed in this way. Amelia has spent many hours developing her understanding of our way of working and transferring it into funding applications and it continues to be our preferred path to growth. This may take slightly longer, however it gives us the opportunity to share the lessons learnt on our projects and our aspirations with people who are prepared to help us clarify our objectives and associated timescales, which holds us accountable.

ACA is continuing to grow organically, sustaining us with sufficient financial resources to give us piece of mind in helping our clients to achieve their projects. Above all, our work is growing in reputation with more people having faith in us. When we first set up, we were conscious that companies such as ours could easily fail in the first three years. Now that we've reached our first ten years, more clients trust us with new projects and challenges in all sectors including collaborations with other architectural and multi-disciplinary Practices.

In the process of writing my first business plan, I recognised the importance of maintaining a holistic approach to design experiences rather than buildings. I recognised that we can only achieve it with a Zen mental attitude dedicating attention to: relationships with the people that will experience our buildings; relationships that our building will establish with the context and the environment; every detail that can influence people's energy flows, particularly of those in need.

One of my first Mental Health projects helped me to understand how different environments affect people differently and I found it a very rewarding discovery. I learnt how our memory events are crucial for our sense of self and can help us to define the purpose and shape of the places we live in. Mental health environments are challenging. In the absence of a clinical background, I dedicated attention to understanding the illness behind the residents' behaviours and their passive withdrawal from the world. This was my first conscious effort to understand how colours, patterns, textures, lighting, sounds and smell could be designed in a way to make people feel safe, reducing their fear and anxiety and facilitating orientation.

In the early days, people (who had no experience of this sector) listening to me passionately talking about these projects would ask me why I enjoyed working in such environments. This made me realise how society influences people to think that people with mental health problems (for instance) can be disposed of just like disused or defective objects in our lives. The risk is that society could discount people that still have something to offer without understanding their dignity or their conditions. I find inspiration for these environments in the meaning of the Lotus flower growing out of muddy waters. At the end of the day all of us need to work with the muddy waters of our imperfections and limitations to flourish through our actions. Wellbeing is a human right, therefore we all deserve an environment that fosters calm and comfort, supporting the healing process when we are ill.

Everything can be recycled in one way or another and it's only a matter of finding the right way and context to reuse something, the same is for me applicable to people. For people to change their lives, they need to find the right relationships and have an environment that allows them to flourish and generate trust in their capacities to help themselves before being able to help others. In the words of Rudolf Steiner, an Austrian Architect and polyhedric cultural figure of the 19th century, *"The humility towards those who are lower than we are, and at whose expense we have been able to rise, must be present everywhere in the world"*.

Although recently our projects have diversified into other sectors, the Mental Health sector still remains at the heart of my interest to understand the transformative mechanism of a physical environment that can help to sooth anxiety, despair and cure psychological or physical illnesses.

Interdependent

Through my meditation and training, I've been working relentlessly on developing my leadership skills with a clear understanding that a creative environment relies on a team's buy-in without room for an ego. What we've achieved over the last ten years couldn't have been by relying solely on my skills or talents, particularly as I wanted to help others. We all have a value and we're all interdependent with infinite possibilities to connect with other people in our lives and work. ACA's broadest mission is to design for wellbeing, expanding our networks and collaborating with anyone or any business who wants to improve the quality of life for themselves or for others.

I've always felt that for our work to have meaning, it needs to be part of an international conversation, to create opportunities to shape innovative environments. We collaborate with several other architectural practices, which could be considered our competitors, either for projects or for being part of similar associations and organisations. When conversations start to flow, we realise just how much we have in common and that the universe provides several opportunities for us all, therefore the focus shouldn't only be on competition. I like to think that we become part of a community invested in the process of innovation, where there's always something to learn from one another, where the quest for excellence isn't driven by the willingness to outdo others, but to embrace change and innovation.

If in the early days of the Practice I was concerned about our model being imitated, writing this book now allows me to totally free myself from any residual concerns of this type. People may emulate a company strategy, but it's difficult to emulate an authentic purpose and culture. I share any trade secrets that I've learnt over the years with colleagues in the office and with the outer world and I find it liberating to focus on the sharing of information to create collaborations that are harmonious.

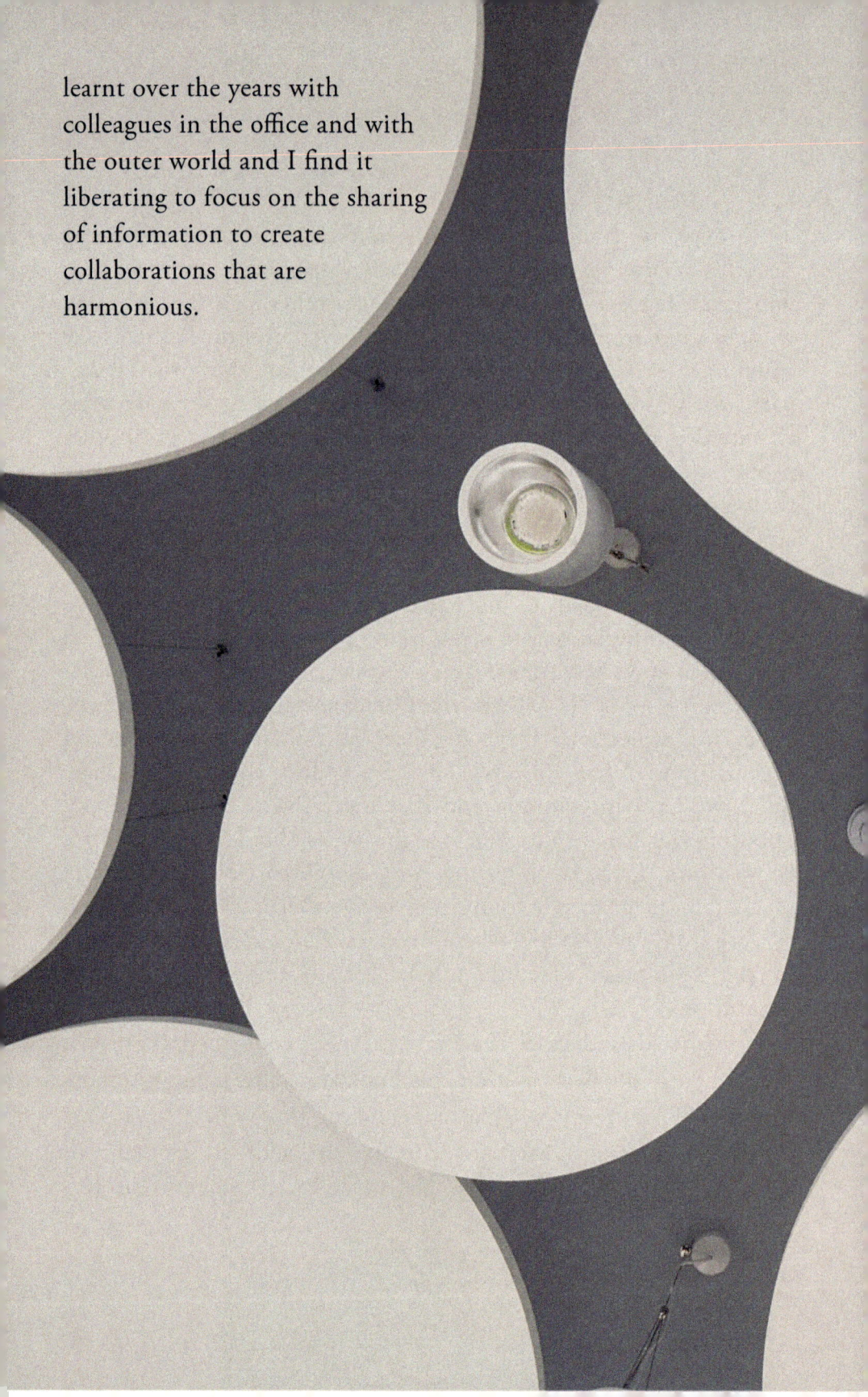

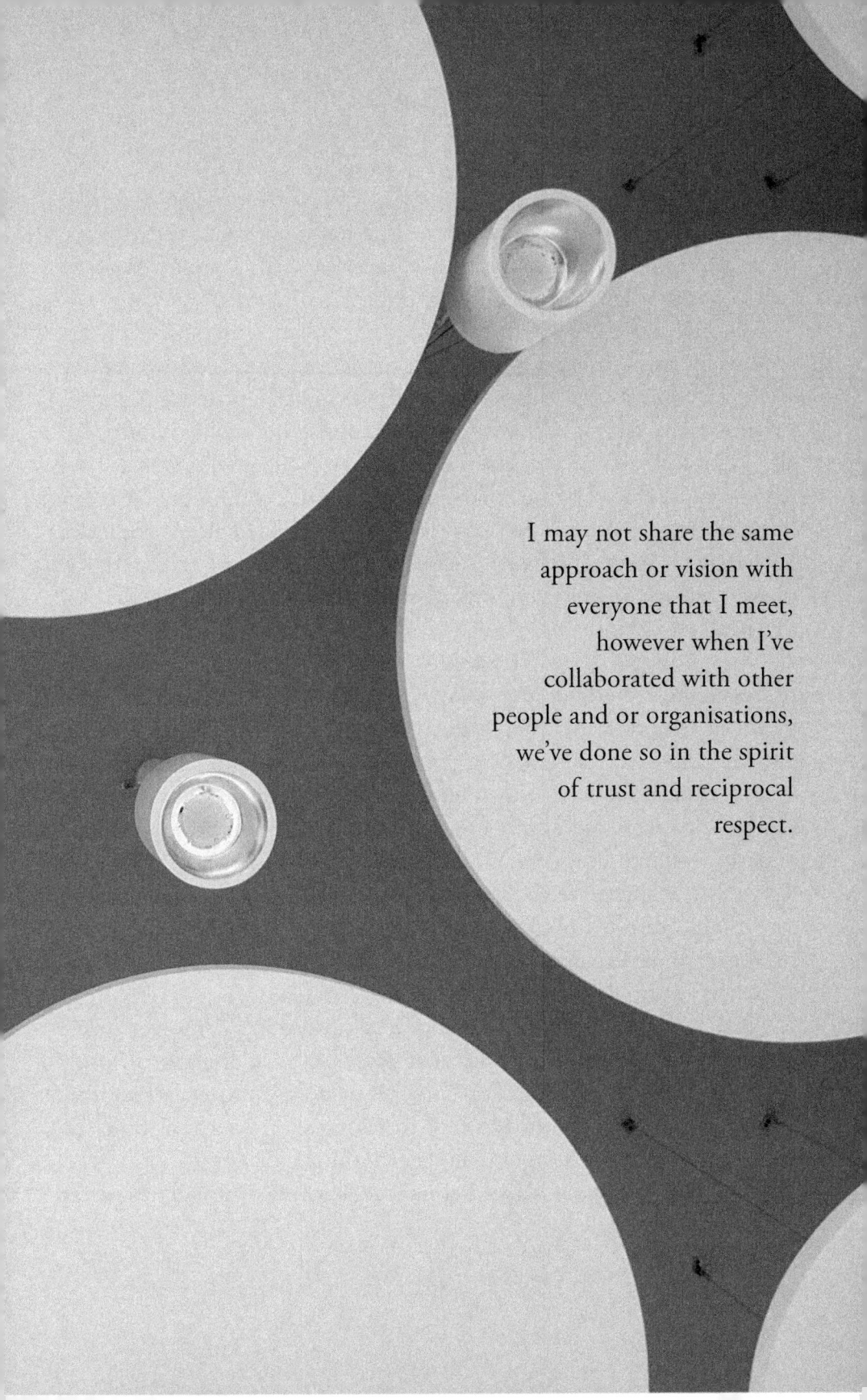

I may not share the same approach or vision with everyone that I meet, however when I've collaborated with other people and or organisations, we've done so in the spirit of trust and reciprocal respect.

The next step

When I left my previous Practice, whether or not I was ready for the next step, I knew I'd have to put my best efforts in to prove to myself that it was the right thing to do to fulfil my aspirations.

As ACA started to grow, we began to measure the quality of our services by requesting regular feedback from our clients. However, we also wanted to look inwards, therefore we signed up to the Mindful Employer charter to dedicate attention to our staff's quality of life. We also hold staff talks on spirituality, health and wellbeing, as well as take part in charitable activities that benefit the local community. I often like to remind myself and others that if we want to achieve excellence in design for wellbeing, we need to start by maximising the strengths of everyone in the team without any individual dominating the process or being left behind.

Our strategy is to grow organically, where the speed of professional growth of our team takes priority over our projects' turnover. We're a small team so most of us need to simultaneously wear multiple hats and everyone is invited to treat our business as if it were their own. The measurement of key performance indicators shared with the team allows everyone to take personal responsibility and understand how the management of projects is progressing. These self-management strategies have allowed us to achieve remarkable results, adopting a flexibility that supports a work-life balance, while maintaining a friendly environment based on solidarity, mutual trust and respect.

Akin to when we meet stakeholders to develop a project brief, everyone is encouraged to find their own voice, be it quiet or loud, to share and challenge ideas on projects or how we run the Practice. This also tests their resourcefulness in taking shared responsibility to lead any projects, with my guidance. In doing so I've fully embraced the powerful words of George Leonard in Mastery: The key to success

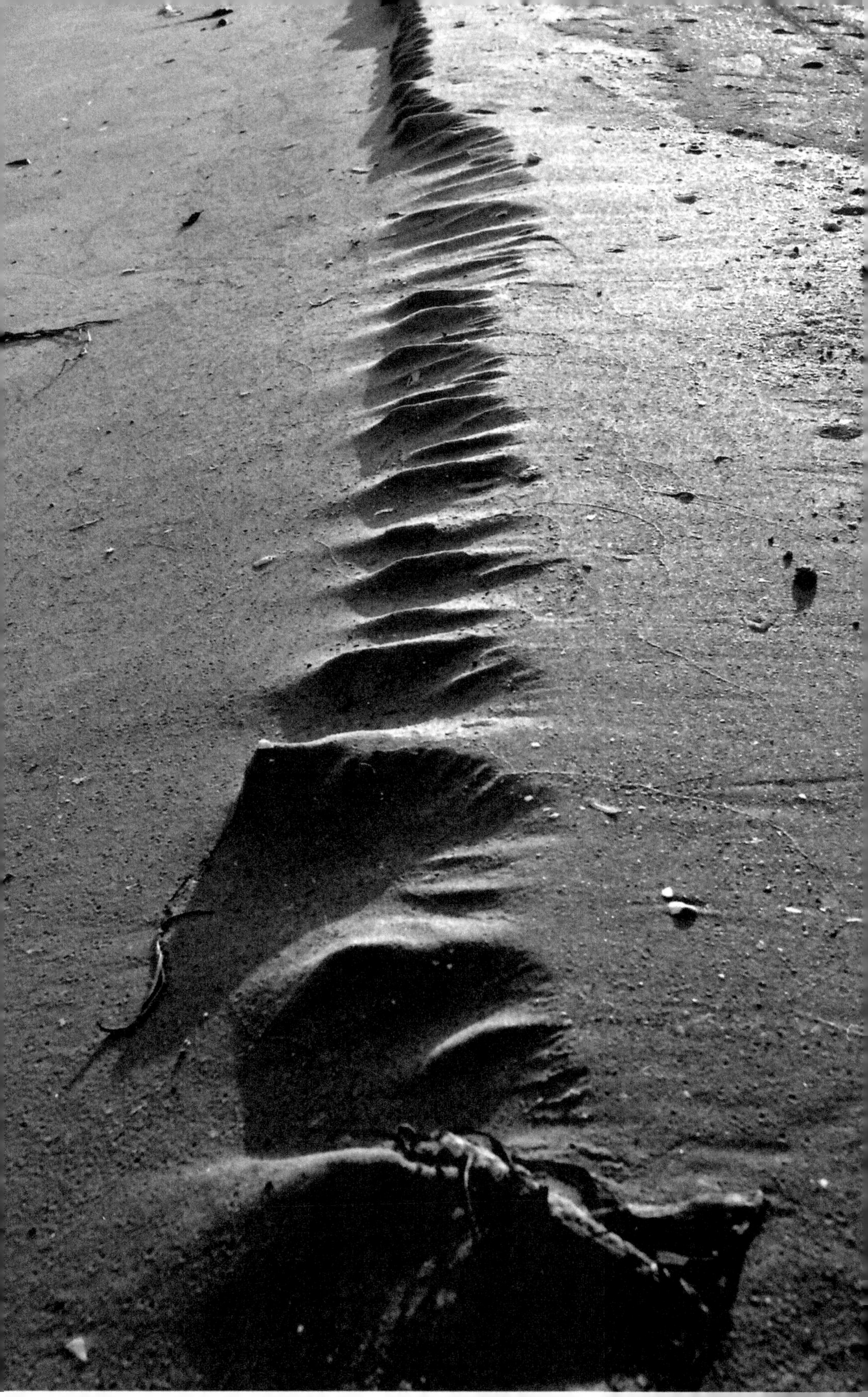

and Long-term Fulfilment: *"Knowledge, expertise, technical skill and credential are important, but without the patience and empathy that go with teaching beginners, these merits are nothing".*

The more effective we are as a team nurturing a creative culture, the more ACA can grow, rewarding team efforts and reinvesting part of the resulting profits. When a new member of the team is interviewed, they are invited to spend up to a day in the office to meet the team before being employed. Everyone has their say in whether they see the new person as a good fit and plays a part in the training or the settling-in process of the new team member.

As the team expands, we're mindful of the risk for personal agendas, that may lead to friction and division within the team. Therefore, we try and keep everyone together by supporting an environment that favours our professional growth, without neglecting our personal spiritual growth, using what makes us individuals to transform ourselves via the interdependence of our working together.

I like the idea of being able to create a comfortable place wherever I feel welcome, so I deliberately avoid having a specific place to practice my Yoga and meditation, just as I don't have a specific place where I work. From the outset, thanks to the use of technology, our work environment has been based on a virtual office model, with an expectation that our team members are disciplined enough with the use of their time when carrying out their work, irrespective of where they work. However, I still prefer it when colleagues choose to come together and work in the office space that we've created; the value of people's interconnectedness can't be underestimated when we are trying to improve people's lives through our designs.

Along with our in-house Continuous Professional Development diary, we have a program that invites members of the team to prepare and share their holiday experiences and personal interests over lunch in a spirit of generosity; it brings people together with a warmth and light-heartedness and helps us celebrate what makes us who we are and our interconnectedness, to inspire our work and expand our horizons. The themes discussed are about belonging, trust, connection, community, security, contentment, authenticity, presence and love; they're all relevant in understanding the needs, desires and habits of the people we design for. The freedom of self-expression at these events and in the office generally allows everyone to feel good and part of a greater whole; these events support the ease of interaction with sincerity and authenticity which don't warrant the need to compete against each other. I see the value in the critical thinking, problem solving, cognitive and creative skills of our team. These events also help us to develop harmonious social skills: to overcome barriers and conflict; to facilitate communication with authenticity (without the need to perform); to understand every situation and every client from a different perspective; to anticipate the client's needs as well as the importance of cooperating with one another. I like to think that retaining a friendly, supportive and empathic work environment provides us with the basis to develop a similar relationship with our community and our planet. Our social media campaign never fails to acknowledge such moments to amplify our team members' voices. Personally, I like to learn how those moments of self-expression influence the way we exercise our judgement of the environments we design.

It doesn't matter whether our work is for people with an illness or their requirement is for an improved environment, I believe that it's part of being human to want to be in a pleasant environment: a well-designed environment can inspire us to live a more fulfilling life and appreciate what is precious in this world and the people we come into contact with.

We're mindful that life is about giving and receiving, therefore every financial quarter, irrespective of the results, we arrange for a social activity with the whole team, as recognition and appreciation of the efforts that go into moving the ACA's projects forward. We hope that in doing so, everyone feels inspired to learn and mentor others in their work, finding satisfaction in doing so, rather than trying to complete a whole project in isolation. One of the teachings I've come across in my meditation is that every teacher should have a minimum of a student and a half. If we can all do so in such a way, any teaching can permeate the universe.

We always conclude projects on site by being mindful of everything we've learnt; simultaneously we start new ones with the same sense of anticipation for the next best project. It's an endless process like any activity in life where we're helping others. The only thing that matters is doing it mindfully of the responsibility to get it right for people and enjoying every part of it, without becoming attached to what has been achieved.

In these moments I remember those childhood moments spent observing the sun's reflections on the sea at different times of the day, feeling the sea breeze while searching for shells washed ashore and hearing the sounds of nature while I laid down on the precarious timber planks I'd managed to place into the Carob tree branches to create a simple shelter. Such memories of nature trigger positive and comforting emotions, which helped me during my hospital stay and still today have the power to make negative experiences fade away. As the Italian novelist Cesare Pavese said: "We do not remember days, we remember moments".

When we can harness nature and the spirit of a location to appeal to our senses and use our sensitivity to re-create the memory of the positive emotions associated with it, our next project, whether for healing, living, working or learning environments, will always give us the opportunity to create a new positive immersive experience. An experience where people feel at home or at ease, contributing to their sense of wellbeing; I love the simplicity of making the most of what the present moment in my learning journey has to offer.

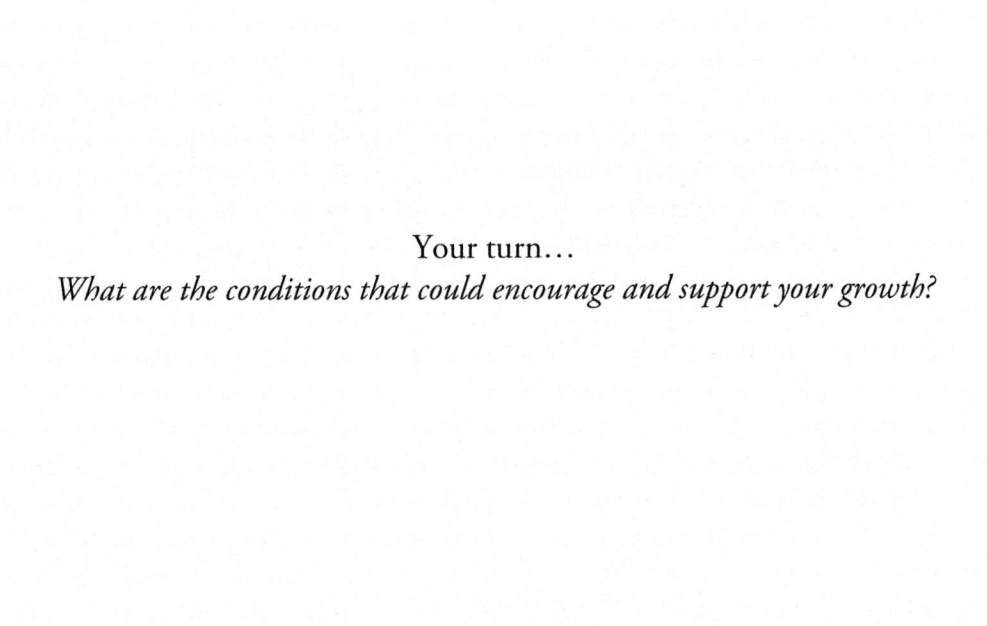

Your turn…
What are the conditions that could encourage and support your growth?

Studio

"We are not going in circles, we are going upwards. The path is a spiral; we have already climbed many steps."

Siddharta, Herman Hesse

Studio, I love this word; Yoga is the study of the combination of meditation and practice, similarly I find my design work to be a combination of meditation and practice. Back in Sicily the family architectural practice was called "studio di architettura" (architecture studio) which in Italian is a name that for me highlights the study required for any architectural design. This was what I based the structure of ACA on, a place where colleagues, construction partners and clients come together to: study what architecture can do for people's lives; practice how to harness the essence of a place; enhance and shape an environment which supports a human experience with positive emotions and fulfil the mission of improving wellbeing in all sectors.

It's a well-known fact that being an architect is one of the longest careers you can aspire to have. Architecture is the endless road to mastery that, like many human activities involving significant learning, is nurtured by: the relationships with people through an empathic curiosity; the creative wellbeing that supports the relationship with our environments; the harmonious language people and the environment share to communicate.

Today I recognise that I've only used my first 25 years in wellbeing design to put in place some foundations and understand the essential and enduring core of this art in my life. My continuous study of the principles at the base of a design for wellbeing is refined through ACA's projects with the aim of positively influencing the lives of as many people as possible. The aim is to make of an ordinary building a transcendent experience empowering people to become whole with their surrounding environments.

This part of the book is the result of reflections on my personal study of a number of readings, conferences talks and spontaneous conversations with fellow speakers as well as conversations with my colleagues in the office and university students who come to spend time with us. Along the way I haven't developed a style or a formula, nor do I intend to develop one, I simply enjoy learning from the design of ACA's projects to gather data for my ongoing investigations.

At a certain point in my journey, I came to a crossroads and the choices I made have influenced the rest of my life with several positive and some challenging lessons learnt along the way. With patience I'm still invested in a gradual learning process to discover what I need to improve in my design for wellbeing through the duality of any inevitable ups and downs.

No matter how serious my accident was, I chose to change the course of my life by expressing my creative energy with positive meditation, daily exercise and trying to improve people's lives through my designs. I believe that my increased sensitivity to pain has given me the best opportunity to understand the sense of euphoria when experiencing a healing environment. With an open mind towards the full range of human experiences, I've learnt that sickness and healing are inseparable and require constant balancing and mindful choices. The ongoing investigation into the perception and observation of other people's feelings through the lens of my own experience, is put into practice through our projects and is observed again through the lenses of the building users. What our body perceives through our senses becomes feelings and these are perceived by our mind; it's therefore important to support our mind with positive feelings, which are derived from a positive perceptual experience of the environment we live in. The understanding derived from such an experiential process is what drives the process towards creative and technical solutions.

I regard the projects I've designed and built over the years as my babies and often go back to see them long after completion to see how they age and adapt to any new challenges beyond what was our initial scope and reach. Above all I'm interested in understanding how the environment created influences individuals' vibrations or frequencies. My ongoing investigation is based on critical questions around the definition of the significance in the essence and integrity of the built form: how can we transform ephemeral feelings from a mental state to a built form? How can design influence interpersonal relationships and with the environment to have a meaningful impact on people's lives? What are the conditions that make a comfortable environment for people?

More than 2500 years ago, the philosopher Pythagoras told his followers that a stone is frozen music and today we know from the basic principle of Quantum Physics that everything is energy in constant motion. Every vibration is equivalent to a feeling that can be positive or negative, which in turn makes our bodies simultaneously a receiver and a transmitter of vibrations that need to be balanced to achieve a harmonious frequency. It's therefore important that we understand the thoughts that hold us back and that we match the frequency of the things we desire. Studies show that the more we move in rhythm with someone, the closer we become to that person. I believe that with our designs, we should seek to achieve a similar match in frequency with the environment to achieve wellbeing.

It's important to acknowledge that we're all connected and the "butterfly effect" implications of any of our actions, however it doesn't mean that we are all living the same reality. I've found practicing Yoga is my way of achieving a detached perspective of my actions and understand more, while resisting the temptation to any comparisons. I'm sure others can achieve the same results with alternative meditative practices, what matters for me is the mindfulness behind the process.

During our life journeys, from when we are born and the years to come, our senses help us perceive the vibrations that inform our growth and change, carrying the deep knowledge of our everyday experiences with our thoughts, the company we keep, the music we listen to, the programs we watch, the atmosphere we find at home or at work, the words we speak and the gratitude we feel for what we achieve and love.

We obtain most of our information through our sight, however it's hearing that connects us most with our environment. According to the Lancet Commission, hearing loss is the largest modifiable risk factor for Dementia and it's not a coincidence that our learning abilities are more affected by our hearing mechanism than problems with vision.

I've developed my career in a country without my native language therefore, I've always found it particularly important to be in environments with soundscapes that facilitate my communication skills. Our ears help us not only to achieve our sense of balance associated to the head's motion in relation to the earth's field of gravity, but also, without directly looking in the direction of the source of a sound, we can hear the resulting sound of a blend of vibrations associated to musical instruments (like a piano, a violin and a guitar) and be able to distinguish each instrument. It's fascinating to understand how airborne sound is transformed into a mechanical stimulation in a solution of water inside the ear that, through the release of chemicals in our body, is converted into electrical signals reaching our brain through nerve fibres.

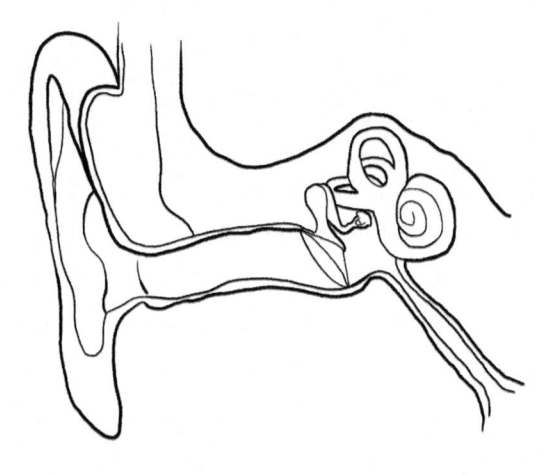

All our senses play a part in the transformation of vibrations that connect us with our environments. I find it important to try and understand the causes and factors that may have caused a degeneration in health in the first instance and explore how the environment designed can be supportive. For example, different molecules are tuned to respond more readily to the vibration of different colours, producing messages that our brain processes to recognise the sensation of the type of colour. Our touch system, through our skin, gives us information on pain, temperature and levels of touch (heavy, medium and light), where the sensitivity of the hair on our skin helps us to tell the difference between a smooth pane of glass and the rough surface of a stone. Through the sense of smell, we can receive molecules that in various combinations can help us perceive up to seven smell-types of odour sensations. Through the sense of taste, depending on the chemical composition and temperature, the molecular interaction allows us to distinguish four main taste buds: sweet, sour, salty and bitter. Not to mention the complex interrelation of ear, nose and throat contributing to our understanding of the environment. We also use our senses to comfort ourselves by looking at photos or scenes of nature, listening to music or natural sounds, smelling candles or flowers, tasting teas or juices and touching rich and warm textures.

The vibrations of our surrounding environment are perceived

through our senses however it's our identity, created by our existential context, that helps us define their frequencies; it's an essential quality of our human existence as distinctive as our fingerprints. Our identity and sense of place, driven by the emotional states experienced in our life, offers unique perspectives of the universe. According to the musician-scientist, Manfred Clynes, *"the qualities of the spectrum of emotions are more precise by far than the words used to describe them."*

Whether via firsthand experience, reading a book or listening to music, we can recognise how each of the seven basic feelings (anger, hate, grief, love, sex, joy and reverence), can manifest themselves through our facial or vocal expressions or the instinctive movements of our bodies.

Clynes suggests that music is the ideal medium to express feelings and communicate emotions simply through the rhythm of the notes, likewise, we all emit a unique frequency. This is also applicable to the buildings and environments we live in, which with their identity, formalised by their shape, form, colour and material, can invite or repel us at a deeper level, while our physical body acts as a receiver of their frequency which goes beyond our sensory system. Quantum physics continues to explore the possibility of a connection between the observer and the observed, between consciousness and the environment, confirming that mind and matter influence each other and that each subatomic particle within us relates to all that is by a unique frequency.

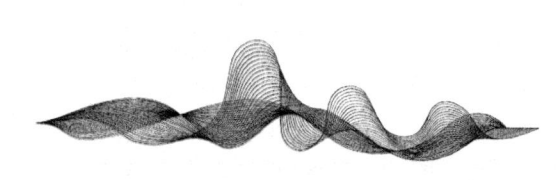

If objects and events are the result of how we perceive the relationship between vibrations, the aim of my design research has been to focus on the mutually dependent and complementary nature of interpersonal relationships and with the surrounding environment, considering that relationships are only possible between different identities. It's been important for me to start this process by understanding the qualities of our identity as human beings; the necessary self-examination of my existential context, recognising my vulnerabilities, has helped me to see the opportunity to transform my life through the tensions and problems encountered but also to understand others to achieve a people-centred design. Recognising my flaws has opened my eyes on how best to address them, for me or others, by way of creating a nurturing environment.

Understanding how to let go of my ego, language and judgement has driven my intentionality to find what is at the base of a happiness frequency that allows us to be in sync with our world to achieve wellbeing. It may well be a purely subjective perspective that I've been willing to explore through the design process with the help of the many people I've met whilst working on ACA's projects.

As part of our design process, we carry out a pre-start survey that is followed up by a post-occupancy survey at the end of the project; both surveys investigate the quality assessment that different building users make of the environment before and after our design. It's been interesting to notice how the people involved in the initial survey usually see a marked difference between the environment before and after our involvement, while those not involved in either surveys may acknowledge the works carried out, without necessarily noticing the difference in the new environment. For me it demonstrates that if we truly want to make the design of the environment part of a preventative medicine strategy, we need to consider that the best medicine is the drug people are happy to take. This highlights the difference in expectations each of us may have in any healing process, as well as the intentionality required to visualise and design an environment that has a positive impact on people. It also reinforces in me the idea that a harmonious frequency is already present in our existential context.

ACA's mission is to collaborate with the project stakeholders' team to shed light and understand the evolving complexity of information required to create a harmonious frequency in the future of their project. It's my responsibility to participate fully in each design adventure to discover how the outcome of my influence can create an innovative environment.

The design of our building environments through their apparent contrast of materiality (shapes, forms, colours and materials), of sensations (inside or outside, day or night, stillness or activity, relaxation or work, independence or community, equality or hierarchy), can be reconciled to offer a harmonious frequency as a guide to interpersonal relationships with the aim of eliminating any ambiguity. We recognise the frequency when all elements of the environment become a music of emotions (associated to the right brain) and causal relationships (associated to the left brain). Whether we sense it or not, the aim is to help people to live a fulfilling and harmonious life characterised by wellbeing, feelings of relaxation and security and enjoying what the present has to offer. In the words on Nikola Tesla *"If you want to find the secrets of the universe, think in terms of energy, frequency and vibration."*

The completed project examples I describe in the following chapters, illustrate how I've applied my study of design, health and wellbeing into practice. My aim is to create a quality of space, which not only provides a shelter that is in harmony with nature, but also improves health and quality of life, with a rich, sensory experience. It's difficult to capture the "experience" of a building with photography, as you need to "feel" the space for yourself, so for this reason, I haven't included too many images of the buildings mentioned. Instead, I hope that my descriptions provide a "holistic" perception of the atmosphere created, as they are influenced by my personal experience, rather than a sum of the perception of each of the senses. I believe that a holistic experience happens when the empathic characteristics of the space designed, makes us feel, without conscious observation.

Our human physiology grants us the remarkable ability to assess our surroundings, whether consciously or subconsciously. However, true comfort extends beyond our physical needs, delving into the realms of psychology and personal perception. The pursuit of designing an ideal environment for a single individual or a group of people presents challenges, but the key lies in creating adaptable spaces that account for the ever-changing climate and environmental context. Our aim is to cultivate a level of comfort that caters for everyone.

To truly influence an individual's perception of a space, it's important to provide freedom of choice and access to sunlight and nature. For instance, the sound of a babbling stream, the gentle whisper of wind through the trees or the soft filters of daylight seeping through the leaves are all powerful natural sources which stimulate our senses. Despite our transition to indoor living, our senses remain attuned to the outdoors. There is no light more invigorating than daylight, no air more refreshing than the breeze outside; we need to extend these natural qualities into the construction of our buildings to achieve a new level of comfort.

Learning from nature, a person-centred, harmonious design can only be achieved by harnessing the collective creativity of a project team to resolve collaboratively how to: do more with less resources; adopt recyclable materials to achieve a closed loop system; reduce waste; rethink the water use and disposal system and adopt natural ventilation, light and climate-adaptive design approaches for the skin of buildings. The end result is a building that efficiently uses natural resources and energy akin to the functions of a thriving ecosystem in a close relationship with its occupants, to improve their health and quality of lives. In the process, we must look beyond the form of the design to feel the essence of our existence. This will provide deeper insights into the present moment and the true nature of our being.

One of the books I loved reading the most, "The Eyes of the Skin" by Juhani Pallasma, highlights the strength of connection between the visual and tactile senses. Similarly, I've found the connection between auditory perception and emotions extremely important in my work. In my experience, architecture can simultaneously stimulate all of the senses to improve people's quality of lives, when designed with this "intentionality". Particularly, I find it fascinating how the omni-directional properties of sound and how our auditory sense, without direct visual contact, allows us to visualise what is happening all around us, triggering a raft of possible emotions. I'm not negating the importance of our visual perception or any of the other senses, rather I'm highlighting the effect an immersive experience, generated by our hearing in relation to air movements or frequencies, allows us to perceive the atmospheric characteristics of a space.

On reflection, I complete many meditative Yoga poses with my eyes closed. The process of blocking out the sounds of early morning tranquillity, interrupted only by birds tweeting as the sun rises, helps me to recalibrate my own being and to remove the blinkers in front of my eyes, to create my own reality. In a similar fashion, during my meditative design process, I focus on alleviating a site context's visual noise to define a new immersive reality for my projects. Compared to Yoga, this is a more pragmatic exercise which still aims to offer an experience integrating people's emotional participation. I find it fascinating how attentive listening allows better understanding in any communication and the role the environment plays in that with its materiality.

The materials I select for our buildings, are not only juxtaposed for

Design & Meditation

visual effect, but also to support the human experience with the understanding of what constitutes a relaxing or harsh soundscape, or the perception of duality of shade and light, in any environment. For example, in one of our projects for St Barnabas Hospice Wellbeing Centre in Boston, we introduced a water fountain as part of the external landscape scheme to mask the surrounding traffic noise. Internally, we suggested a low-level nature sound to enrich the nature-inspired, multi-sensory, interior design experience to camouflage the cumulative noise of people talking in the open, communal areas. It was an attention to a rather immaterial detail that aimed to bring awareness to one of the senses that can't be overlooked when creating a multi-sensory and immersive experience. I find fascinating to research the unassuming simplicity of details based on the understanding of the properties of different materials and as Mies van der Rohe once said: *"We must remember that everything depends on how we use a material, not on the material itself"*.

A harmonious language

I could say that I learnt my first "second language" as soon as I started attending school, as Sicilian (unlike Italian) is in fact, a spoken language of its own, which one picks up on the street, rather than being taught at school. During my high school studies, I was taught to read and translate Latin and English. Although there was very little time dedicated to speaking skills, I gained an idea of how languages differ in structure and an opportunity to understand cross-cultural insights and observations. After university, when I went to live in Madrid, my knowledge of Latin helped me to quickly learn the basics in Spanish and my rudimentary English allowed me to communicate with friends when I moved to the United Kingdom.

I soon realised that speaking multiple languages slows down the communication process in any context, it's not uncommon in any culture to blame foreigners for their stupidity or craziness; however, I've always focused on the blessing of having more options to consider, while trying to understand or speak another language.

If the experience of my accident had influenced my determination in being more intentional in design for wellbeing, I believe that experiencing a variety and diversity of foreign environments has opened my mind and ability to learn differently, by processing different perspectives that can influence my perception of the world in ever-evolving ways. It's a rewarding experience that has fuelled a deeper interest in understanding people's cultures and behaviours and how they may interpret my behaviour, more than the words used. It's a communication process like the one we experience with the environment.

Through my study of Neuroscience associated to architecture, I've discovered that the experience of living in Italy, Spain and England as well as speaking each language has impaired my language fluency. I recognise that my brain is often trying to communicate with competing words associated to dominant and non-dominant languages in real time. Having long ago accepted the disadvantage of my speed of expression, it was reassuring to learn that there are also advantages: multiple language speakers are able to be present, flexible and sensitive in a specific context and express themselves in multiple ways.

It made sense to try to harness these skills to become more effective in walking in the shoes of the people we design for to find a common harmonious language between people and our planet; to understand what are the qualities of the environment that engage people's senses to support wellbeing. Years of study have convinced me that the work put in understanding oneself can unlock the understanding of other people's perspectives. I'm not talking about an egocentric view of the world, rather adopting the awareness of self to pay attention to those details of other people's lives, through contrasts and differences in perspectives.

The capacity human beings have to adapt and to interact with their environment is what makes them feel alive. By contrast, failing to do so would mean being dead. I've realised that the relationship between people and their environment is like the relationships between people. In both types of relationships, I like to spend time understanding the intentional verbal and symbolic expressions and those unintended and symptomatic. In both cases, clear and simple communication between the two parties require painstaking amounts of care for the content, rhythm and pace.

The atoms and molecules that make up physical matter vibrate with energy and their frequency defines the state in which they appear to us: solid, liquid or gas. In nature, everything is vibration and the vibration of certain frequencies becomes a perceptual and visual language that is based on geometries and shapes, colours, motions, numbers, angles, proportions and sounds.

Our human energy systems are affected by various factors that include our emotions and our relationships with others. As we age, our memories may fade. However we tend to remember most of our feelings in response to certain life experiences. We perceive our reality as we match its energy vibration. For example, the average human ear can only detect soundwaves with frequencies ranging from 20 to 20,000 vibrations per second, yet there is a far wider range of sounds that we can't hear.

Energy comes in three forms: inherited, absorbed from food and from our surroundings. Our emotions are a reflection of the environment's energy frequency; therefore the design of our environments should offer a harmonious sensory perception that supports a positive state of mind. A thoughtful design of our environments could be a critical part of a preventative medicine strategy, supporting positive adaptations in the day-to-day process of living. The design adds value to people's lives with a harmonious language, which balances intentionality and action.

Languages such as Italian and English are rather different. When I first arrived in England, during the "culture shock" stage, while I tried to make sense of what was different from my own country, my senses were bombarded with a raft of new places, smells, materials and in some situations, the language was more like a blur of sounds. In the learning process, I started to recognise the sounds associated to words that fitted the context and meaning of the conversation. Nowadays I can even recognise different English accents.

I find the mastering of a design process very similar to the mastering of a new language, in that the initial blurred vision of a new project for a client, through the learning process allows us to recognise the materials that fit the cultural context and the pattern required to give the project concept meaning. I find it fascinating to explore how geometry manifests in nature along with the pattern of materials and colours, to deliver a simple and intuitive accent of communication, which is grounded in the local context. Such an alchemic process is complete when the space is congruent with its function, supporting a close relationship between people's culture and the environment in which they participate, to achieve wellbeing.

Language can be independent of words. For me, the sketches of each project become a silent language, where every detail stands for something due to instinctive impulses and emotional perceptions, giving a meaning to what is unsaid. In a way it's knowing everything without consciously listening to anything. The design process becomes an exercise in reduction and searching for simplicity without compromise.

The study of geometric, structural forms from Greek to Islamic and more recent Contemporary architecture, plays an important influence in my work, as they all adopt geometry to understand the world. Likewise, the study of geometric forms I adopt for ACA's buildings often seek inspiration from the study of the context (natural or urban), to achieve a gradual metamorphosis with the conscious aim of establishing a precise emotive relationship with people. It's the spontaneous and intuitive search to discover what is attractive about a place that becomes part of the ever-evolving language of each project; the result of the interaction between creativity and the project stakeholders' emotional perception. It's an evolving process of communication, a continuous exchange between the environment, the senses and emotions and vice versa, until it becomes a harmonious language which embraces the vibrational energy of the context.

My role in the process is to be sensitive to what is happening in people's lives (that we are designing for) and to understand their sensory experience. It's like holding up a mirror in front of them to help visualise and shape the quality and intensity of a fresh, multi-sensory spatial experience that supports a positive change in their lives.

According to Werner Heisenberg, a German Theoretical Physicist: *"the observer alters what he observes by the mere fact of his observation"*. Therefore, one single reality doesn't exist. In the design process, my aim is to support not only interpersonal communication between people, but also between people and the environment; exploring the interrelationship between their kinaesthetic (body knowledge) and visual experience of a space, capable of creating a bespoke whole reality for the observer and the observed. It's an ever-changing language, which for some projects can become very specialised, due to specific adaptations required to support certain people's conditions.

I embrace the idea that all things are related to one another, so understanding the role our senses play in the communication process with a space is for me, the most exciting adventure. The multi-directional and multi-dimensional perception of distance receptors (such as eyes, ears and nose) and immediate receptors (like touch) are influenced by our cultural backgrounds, which determine what we screen out or what we pay close attention to. Everything we do as human beings occurs within a space. Therefore, an individual's lifetime memories need to be considered to reactivate their positive emotions and to support different levels of social relationships (private, semi-private or public), which is applicable to all sectors.

Passion and emotion, integral to our psychic existence, are the waves that unite self and the world. They emerge as our responses to the environment's relentless pressures, demanding our attention to their voices and demands. Engaged in a participatory dance with the universe, the individual reacts uniquely, constantly enriched, stirred, and propelled by exchanges with the outer realms. This interplay epitomises the essential duality of consciousness and perception.

The perception of our world is a function of our culture, relationships, activities and emotions and we should harness the influence a building can have on people. Like when eating, we should chew the food long enough to perceive its taste, the design of our environment should allow for our pace to slow down enough to mindfully appreciate the energy that can influence us and a way to appreciate the flow of life.

Communication is like a dance, when the listener and speaker are engaged as one, so is the design of an environment where content is only a minor part of communication, which is developed to generate emotions with purpose, so that people are aware of them and consider how to react. It's usually the reactions that create challenges, not the emotions themselves.

We are all creatures of emotions, thoughts and desires and like in most relationships, our building design should aim to achieve a harmonious language to create a compassionate and engaging environment, offering people endless opportunities to link in with past experiences and supporting their emotions. The quality of ACA's buildings, independently if they are for living, studying, working or healing, aim to adopt a language that makes people feel appreciated, supporting their intuitive orientation with a thoughtful colour strategy that influences their electromagnetic field and meaningful symbols grounded in the local cultural context. The resulting building should provide a social space for people to spend quality time together, within a multi-sensory and immersive experience that touches individuals; it should support a relationship with the environment that helps to correct people's energy imbalances.

In the words of the Spanish Artist Pablo Palozuelo, whose work and readings have had a significant influence on my work since my time in Madrid: *"Space, an unlimited ocean, is the matrix of all signs and rhythms. Space lives the life of space, it is the substance of thought, the transparency of the waters"*.

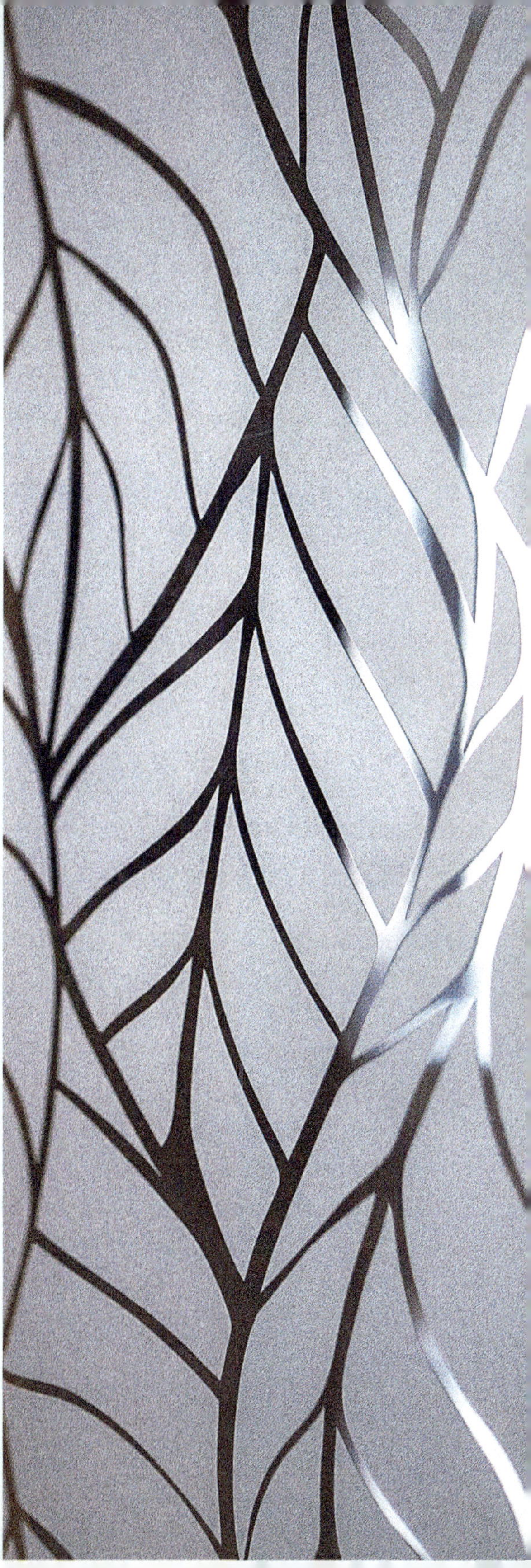

Empathic Curiosity

The aim of my journey has been to learn to worry less about how people feel about me in favour of learning how I can make people feel through the design of a building environment that offers a physical and psychological shelter. We're all connected by the "butterfly effect" embedded in our planet and it's important to establish authentic and empathic relationships, to understand and share the feelings of another person. The relationships between people and the environment are like the relationships between people and we should learn from it.

One of the most interesting things I've learnt through my readings about neuroscience, self-tested through my meditation, is that we are the creators of our realities and we're capable of creating a different response even when focusing on the same apparent truth with incomplete information. Our brains are provided with mirror neurons that fire when we observe the same action performed by another person; the question I've been researching is whether it's possible to create an environment that can trigger these neurons by way of influencing the people using the building. How can a building design influence people's brain chemical composition, balancing hundreds of neurotransmitters like dopamine, serotonin and cortisol? How can the design of the environment trigger pleasurable feelings such as comfort and support to a point where people feel happy with limited stressors? Can influencing some people be sufficient to encourage a group response in a building that remains versatile for a sufficiently large number of different people during its time?

The opposing ebbs and flows of dopamine and serotonin make us all different; the different proportions of introvert and extrovert personalities may affect the result the building has on each person. Only the people that use the building can provide us with significant feedback. My focus is on developing the brief to understand what makes people feel good. Finding positive solutions for people during this stage has an effect on me, the release of dopamine derived by this process creates the conditions to support my learning. It's the realisation of a symbiotic and sensitive insight that allows me to connect with the building users while understanding how they process situations and the building environment.

Years ago, I recall that during the early stages of brief development for Townend Court, a Learning Disability Inpatient Services development on behalf of Humber Teaching NHS Foundation Trust, every time I visited the old ward, I could particularly hear one of the residents in distress. People with learning disabilities can have severe challenging needs associated to comorbidities such as mental health problems, autistic spectrum disorder, multiple disabilities and communication difficulties with risks to themselves and others. Spending time on the ward was both enlightening and enjoyable with good banter between the management and nursing team I was working with. During some of the meetings with the Nurse Team I had the pleasure of meeting Hannah, one of the residents, and through the interpretation and communication of the nurses, (she couldn't join in the conversation due to limited communication skills) I gained a real insight into Hannah's story and the challenges of the environment she experienced.

Along the way, I've learnt about the transformation of care for learning disabilities throughout history from the institutionalised care of the 1930's, focusing on segregation and separation, to present day care, focusing on ordinary community living with personalised support. The old building was more akin to the 1930's model despite the caring team's best efforts to make residents feel at home. There was a looping long central corridor without any windows, natural light nor restorative views outside; outdoor areas with fencing resembling a mental institution and the bedrooms lacked en-suite facilities. It didn't strike me as an ideal place for living, never mind healing.

The new building design provides a welcoming entrance with large, glazed areas that allow people to see inside, reducing the feeling of resident segregation for those who have family members staying there. The choice of outdoor areas offers variations in form and daylight, with a discreet enclosure, camouflaged by the bespoke landscape scheme. In terms of layout, the building facilitates the model of care and residents' pathway, from admission to treatment and rehabilitation, with communal areas supporting autonomy, social interaction and stimulation. For staff, it also facilitates natural observation and ease of circulation. Additionally, the communal areas provide recognisable variations in the quality and geometry of the rooms, including vaulted ceilings with different heights and shapes. Above all, the interior design strategy supports a comfortable environment, with use of colours and materials providing sound attenuation, which facilitates intuitive orientation and promotes wellbeing.

Part of the brief was to design an extra care room to facilitate the care of residents during distress. When the new building was complete, the new environment had produced such a positive effect on residents, that the extra care room has rarely been used.

At a conference to share the results of the completed building with the healthcare specialist design community, the Nurse Team had filmed the residents in their new environment. It was a joy to watch how proudly they showed off their "new home" and rewarding feedback for the collaborative work undertaken to understand the unmet residents' needs. However what counted most was to discover that our brains can be moulded by different experiences and can adapt to different situations, even for people with learning disabilities for instance, whose conditions affect their perspectives differently.

~ ~ ~

Working through the memories of my early life, I recall discussions with my family about art and creativity. Yet, as for many people, when it came to emotions, they were demonstrated more by expressions of love rather than openly discussed. It was more important to get on with life without the need to dwell on the feelings associated to it. Although I was sensitive to other people's emotions, when it came to myself, I seemed to pay more attention to direct criticism rather than positive emotions. Perhaps I'd always been sensitive, but my motorbike accident and resulting stay in hospital has heightened this trait. Through this experience, I've become more aware of others' feelings and an avid active listener, who recognises other people's body language, pauses and micro-expressions, to understand how I can help.

I like to discover the significance in the project at hand and believe that this sensitivity has enhanced my creative skills to seek an appropriate design response in line with what a situation or person requires.

I've always been curious about new ideas, situations and what people see or feel through my work; it's a way of living that can't be switched off. I've become more mindful to understand people, how they work or live, as well as their personalities and preferences. Thinking through people's design requirements or pondering about building information received, helps me to consider options on how our designs can help. Therefore, I use my meditative practice to process how to find a solution to people's design requirements, whilst keeping objective and emotionally detached from any anguish people in healthcare environments may experience. What I love most about the brief development is the intriguing process that helps me to untangle different aspects and ambiguities of a project; technical and regulatory areas of concern blend in with the character traits of the people we are designing for. At ACA, we work our way through this process with the help of environmental assessment tools which we've developed to be bespoke for different types of buildings. This is an informal observation structure, developed to genuinely understand the details of people's activities that provide value and meaning to their lives. We use this as a base for conversations with a variety of stakeholders which offer different perspectives, helping us to see a pattern in the environment people are living in, be it harmonious or threatening. Through conversations, questions and collaborative critical thinking we try to understand how stakeholders' human experiences can help us capture what may be missing in their lives. Can our designs provide a greater empathic story which considers values such as dignity, diversity, responsibility, community, creativity and innovation?

Although we all have different ways of perceiving the environment and processing information, sensitivity is a trait that is common in most of us and helps us reconcile with the world, while engaging our emotions and senses; the materiality of our body interacts with the physical quality of the environment. My personal experience of a care environment has influenced my design specialism in the years that followed, providing me with a focus on understanding what the needs of our hearts are and the most appropriate sensory conditions for a design response that allows people to instinctively recognise a comfortable environment; providing them with positive experiences that offset any negative ones associated to their past.

I found this particularly important when designing Dementia care environments where comfort, love and respect are the essential conditions for people to live a supportive experience; when regions of our brains may be affected in the reading of signals received from our senses, which are often affected detrimentally by comorbidities.

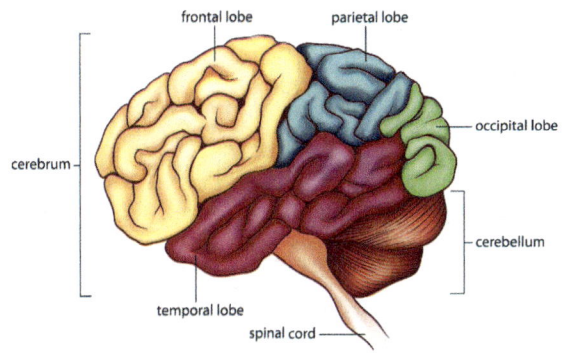

To deepen my understanding of this condition, I've studied the three brain regions, which are based on the quantity and length of exposure to our experiences in life. The first region is the brain stem connected to the spinal cord and helps to regulate essential living functions such as breathing, heart rate and body temperature, which don't vary substantially in different environments. The second is the brain region (Parietal, Temporal and Occipital Lobe) which is connected with what our senses learn from the environment we've experienced in our early lives. The third is the frontal lobe region, which is critically connected with our life experiences and characterises human adaptability associated with reasoning, motor skills, higher level cognition, and expressive language. In particular, the type of cognitive decline associated to Dementia depends on the types of neurons and regions of the brain affected.

The question for me is: how can we create a supportive and heart-warming environment that is engaging for different parts of the brain so that we can retain cognitive functions for as long as possible?

To respond to this question, over the years ACA has deliberately offered Interior Design services to create holistic experiences, ensuring that a caring message is carried out from the external building's appearance to the indoor environments. For this reason, our design is mostly developed from the inside out. Primarily, we develop an understanding of how room adjacencies influence staff workflows and residents' care pathways, to provide an environment that satisfies everyone's deepest human needs. The aim is to achieve an environment that makes everyone feel appreciated, whatever their backgrounds, supporting people to regain balance and control of their health and conditions in a subliminal way. The end result is an empathic design of an environment which offers people endless opportunities for engagement, acknowledging personal past experiences and supporting emotions.

Externally, protective boundaries need to be well-defined as a physical limit, like a solid wall to protect people, with a clear line of sight, ensuring staff and residents feel safe for self and others. On the contrary, indoors, boundaries are more fluid and can be defined with a variety of details, such as a small cluster of chairs around a fireplace, inviting people to socialise. What counts is to communicate a homely place where people can relax and feel safe, to restore their balance.

A few years ago, I developed the interior design of Fern House Independent Living on behalf of Abbeyfield for people who are over 55 years of age. Designed to host multiple services, the building comprises of two wings dedicated to apartments and one wing dedicated to a care home, which offers additional care and support, when the residents' circumstances change.

I enjoyed collaborating with the Care Team to design an environment supportive for "Sally and John", a story of two residents typically using the building. Sally and John had been friends for several years and when Sally was first diagnosed with Dementia, John used to visit her every day in her own home, before her condition deteriorated and she required extra care.

Sally's family had to make in their words "an agonising decision" to move her into a care environment, as she was no longer capable of living independently at home. They were concerned because although she was in the family home, she kept asking to go home and called out for beloved pets who had long since passed away. The pain and upset this caused Sally and her family indirectly was distressing.

Following Sally's move into the completed development, the family mentioned that the difference in Sally's behaviour was remarkable; she had stopped asking to go home, no longer called out for her lost pets and she smiled more often. The only missing link was her friend John. Initially, he came to visit and have lunch with Sally every day, until the commute became too much. So, he eventually moved into one of the apartments in the same building.

Sally's family added that since their Mum started living in the new building where she can have her hair done in the salon, wander into the

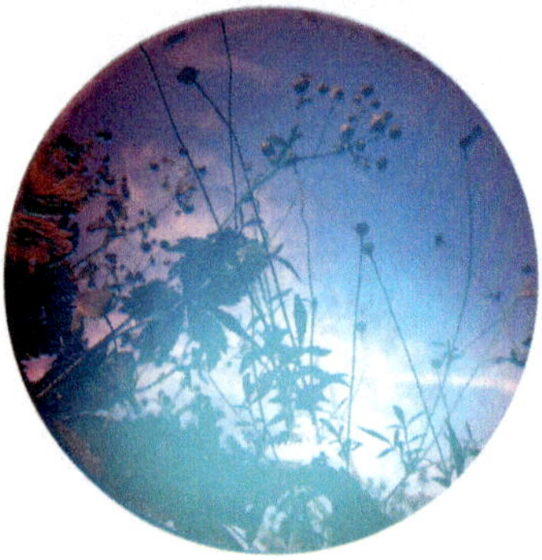
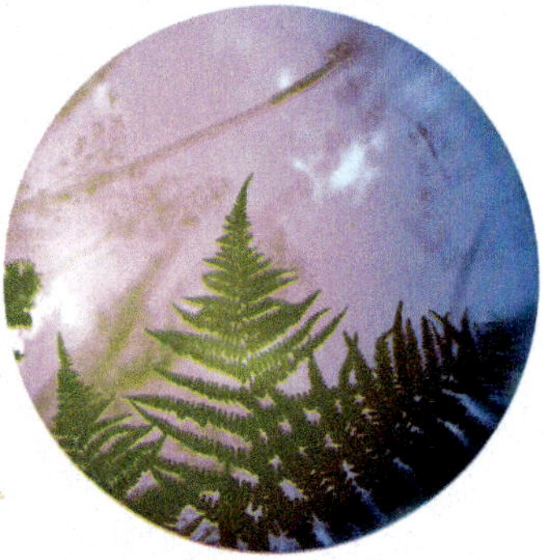
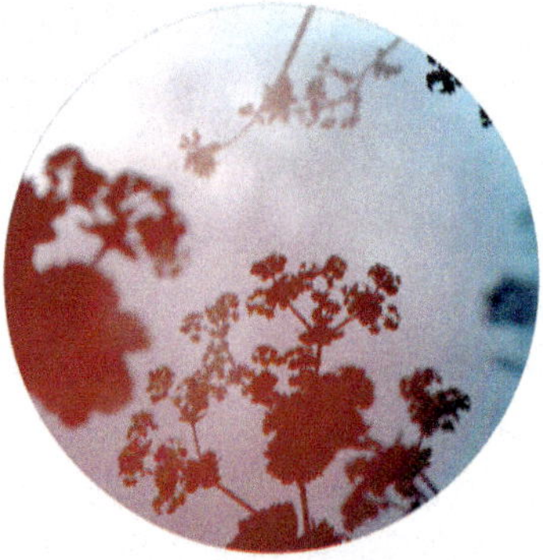

shop to buy snacks and eat in the restaurant with John; her quality of her life has improved and her levels of distress and anxiety have reduced.

The story of Sally and John influenced me to design an environment that can adapt to different people and situations; some people simply aging and wanting to downsize, some with early-onset Dementia and some showing a higher degree of acuity of needs. Each person is on their own journey and requires something different from their environment, hence crafting a space with an interior design strategy that meets each person's needs and expectations is always an important challenge to embrace.

The extra care environment was designed not for the way it would look, but as a multi-sensory narrative to help people regain balance and facilitate a sense of environmental control. It was particularly important to understand how to support the creation of a multi-cultural environment and how best to adapt the environment to people's rich vocabulary of scent, texture, taste, sight and sounds. Like me, as I mentioned earlier in this book, we all reminisce about familiar places and people that have made us feel happy; what is close to our hearts provides comfort. Therefore, we selected warm materials and fabrics with comfortable textures; tactile art installations and vintage handcrafted objects and images that connect people to their memories. Colours were chosen to support an uplifting atmosphere and to help people navigate with their instinct by the change in the electromagnetic field around them. Every aspect of the environment was designed to meet each person's needs, to offer a sense of well-being, to revive an interest in the world and give hope.

Also, the environment was designed to support people's abilities to function independently, as this is connected to an improved sense of self and well-being: every space has a small cluster of simple furniture with comfortable curves that facilitate a sense of intimacy and proximity; good quality acoustics help people to discern what they hear; the visual connection to landscaped areas is supported by the difference in natural light and where this isn't possible, it is enhanced by the warm colours of a natural scene backlit image. The power of a simple window goes beyond providing light, it provides something more intangible: a point of reference, a distraction from the place or a space to sit nearby and meditate.

Behaviour support strategies were at the heart of every detail decision process to ensure accessibility for those using mobility aids, those with sensory impairments and those with limited dexterity. The communal areas were completed with a warm and soothing fireplace for people to gather around; a piano for talented players, a reminiscence area with a screen, books and a photo display which connected to people personal lives. The small kitchen emanates scents, transporting residents to the comfort of the past, through the choice of food and drinks prepared and served in the dining area where residents meet. The choice of alternative spaces creates opportunities for people to engage with each other or simply to recall memories and atmospheres.

For this project I worked with a talented local artist for the selection of vintage copper kettles which, due to their use, show comfort in their imperfections and provide an engaging display without the constraints of fragility. Furthermore, they provide a strong connection with people's stories of the locality, stimulating emotional curiosity and conversations about one of the most memorable activities popular in our country: enjoying a nice cup of tea!

The variety of environmental qualities was critical to provide a space where it's possible to live with the symptoms of Dementia, from the early stages. The extra care apartments were tailored to aid couples, where one of them may be experiencing early-onset symptoms of Dementia, allowing families to live together as long as possible and considering the rich, fulfilled lives that people have experienced, with a respectful and dignified place to live.

The harmony of all spaces was achieved gradually and collaboratively by examining emerging, common traits with empathy, to continuously improve our attention to detail, while considering the several perspectives of the people using the environment created. The heart of our design is to create an environment that supports people's needs and to facilitate the perception of features which can empower them to navigate their environments intuitively, particularly when the level of perceptual abilities is low.

~ ~ ~

Throughout my studies into how the brain works, I've learnt that before we can decide what to do next, our brain needs to process what's happening in the present moment. Interestingly, most of us are prone to using the left side of our brains (associated to verbal and analytical skills) more than the right (associated with our visual and intuitive skills) and my curiosity has been mainly aimed at understanding the influence our environments have on our behaviour and perceptual sensitivity based on people's experiences.

I'm interested in the nonverbal communication that people's senses can intuitively receive in any environment: how different colours help us to move (kinetics); how the tactile properties of materials help us to perceive (haptics); how to use a space (proxemics); how the environment can influence the way we speak (vocalics); how we use our time (chronemics) or how we engage in social interactions through the use of our sense of smell (olfactics). Our response to a space isn't limited to our senses, much lies within the magical chemical process of the hormones orchestrated by our brains, based on our experiences! Purpose triggers the release of dopamine, relaxation comes from serotonin, endorphins are activated by exercise, and oxytocin is released by love and connection. They're all critical factors that can influence our levels of happiness and our immune systems and they require consideration when designing a holistic experience to support people's wellbeing.

For example, the relatively recent trend of single-bed rooms compared to multiple-bed rooms in early hospitals, (of which I've had personal experience), has demonstrated an improvement on limiting the spread of infection. However, this trend has increased a patient's sense of isolation which, particularly in the older population, contributes to a decline in their immune responses. Studies have demonstrated that the way we perceive colours can be influenced by our experience biases, depending on whether people are early risers or night owls, which is due to the way natural light exposure influences their lives. When designing the number and orientation choice of bedrooms in hospitals and care homes, it's important to provide options to cater for both early risers and night owls; it's equally important to provide a variety of spaces for positive social interactions, to uplift patients' spirits.

As we are all unique, it's important to ensure that people-centred design features support all of our brain functions, with subliminal instructions that help us to respond well to the environment, reducing stress and anxiety. Therefore, the idea that "one size fits all" doesn't apply to our designs irrespective of the sector: healthcare, education, residential or commercial. For instance, working in an open-plan office doesn't suit everybody, neither does learning in large groups in educational settings, however the environment can help people to overcome any deficits in their perception of the situation. What is crucial is that the building-user perceives a soothing space, which enhances their sense of wellbeing.

Each of our projects help us to understand: how people respond to the architectural features proposed; what are the environmental characteristics that attract people's attention; what makes them choose or avoid a particular behaviour (influenced by their past experiences) and with what effect.

My studies into how our brains process complex, social interactions and understand other people's emotions has unveiled that our brains consciously process how we feel through information coming from our senses and subconsciously receives signals transmitted by our major organs. For example, when noise levels increase, our heart rates increase simultaneously. Specifically, David Robson, author of The Intelligence Trap explains: "There is growing evidence that signals sent from our internal organs to the brain play a major role in regulating emotions... Much of the processing of these signals takes place below conscious awareness... the way you read and interpret those feelings will have important consequences for your wellbeing."

The idea that our logic processes follow our emotions, perceived by organs such as the heart and the gut, is a powerful demonstration of how the look and feel of our environments stimulate the senses following the function; it's an opportunity to create a memorable environment which helps people to communicate, to learn, to entertain and to socialise.

~~~

In my studies, I've learnt that the first sign of civilisation in an ancient culture, according to the anthropologist Dr. Margaret Mead, was an animal's healed, broken bone, because it demonstrated that someone had taken care of the animal in question. Equally today, we should still have the responsibility to dedicate time in understanding what people need and feel, to design a recovery-focused environment.

Throughout my journey, I've worked on a variety of Mental Health projects, including Medium and Low Secure Units as well as Locked/Open Rehabilitation developments. The service-users I've met have had a variety of issues, which haven't always been obvious to detect. A few years after completion, I returned to visit Priory Hospital Middleton St George Women's Medium Secure Unit I designed, along with the Hospital Director, to understand how the environments had evolved. I sat in the lounge with a number of service-users and found it difficult, in some cases, to distinguish the nurses from the resident service-users, while they freely offered me feedback on which parts of the building they liked to spend time in the most. For me, it proved that the right environment allows everyone to flourish.

My experience designing such Mental Health environments has provided me with the opportunity to develop an understanding of the recovery process required to support people to build a more fulfilling,

Design & Meditation

meaningful and satisfying life for themselves. The combination of a well-designed, physical environment and a therapeutic culture with healing opportunities are all important in facilitating a successful recovery journey. A recovery-focused environment needs to be "inclusive" and allow the person to have choice and more active control over their life; encouraging skills development and discovering a sense of personal identity.

Recovery begins with hope. Along with clinical teams and the service-users, as designers we have a responsibility to create buildings and environments which inspire and maintain hope, as well as providing a safe place to live. Hope is the bedrock upon which we build our recovery!

ACA's projects completed in this sector provide environments that support hope and motivation, maximising opportunities for social engagement, peer support, and partnership working; recovery is unlikely to happen in isolation. Service-users need opportunities to engage with each other and with those who are supporting them.

The environments we create are often open-plan with natural light and good air circulation; a central hub Bistro/Café type area provides a shared communal space that maximises engagement and the development of supportive relationships. Mental health recovery is characterised by peaks and troughs; therefore, we design the environment with a flexible layout that allows carers to deal with a range of complex behaviours during wellness and relapse.

In direct contrast to the stereotype of a clinical and sterile Psychiatric hospital, ACA's designs favour a high-quality, homely environment as a major factor capable of influencing responses to stress and anxiety, smoothing the transition from what residents would experience at home. The conflict between security versus homeliness will always be there, so we work with clinical teams open to exploring fresh and simple solutions, whilst managing published guidance and regulations. Modern, safe kitchens and suitable laundry facilities are an important part of recovery, so they are located to support the service-user training programme in the use of domestic equipment, so they can regain confidence when returning to a life in the community.

The main communal space of Priory Lichfield Road, a community facing rehabilitation and recovery service, is also the entrance to the facilities. It's an important design feature, like a piazza, that can help users see a progression in their journey from segregation to ordinary living in the community. The location of this facility within the layout also plays an important role as it communicates autonomy and openness to the local community as well as social interaction and stimulation. The sensory experience of the communal area with different spaces and shapes helps to create opportunities for groups to congregate rather than being an intimidating, large space. The central location of the kitchen acts as a focal point of scents that may help with restoring positive daily routines. Light, texture and colours are all used to create an inviting environment while noise reduction strategies help to reduce reverberation that may disorient people. They are all elements of design created to achieve a balanced environment.

I don't view the service-users' core needs any differently to my own: a building which is dark, cold, poorly-designed, and uninspiring is not only going to negatively impact anybody's emotional state, but also hinder recovery.

The environments described proved to make the services-users feel valued, maintain dignity, promote personal responsibility, develop self-esteem, self-worth and increase their feelings of happiness. They are all light and impalpable emotions!

Mental health is often associated with social malfunction, yet perhaps it could also be understood as the perception of emotions without filter. On the other hand, creativity is a mixture of many emotions, so I believe that with a solution-focused approach, the environment can help people to be themselves and reduce the stigma attached to mental illness.

~~~

Following my accident, my life has been significantly and consistently shaped by the curiosity of how people feel in their contexts. ACA's projects aren't limited to just one sector or scale of projects, what they have in common is a curiosity that facilitates learning and fuels my mission to help people find clarity where there is ambiguity. The project examples described earlier in this chapter focus on environments requiring a high degree of empathic curiosity to understand people's life challenges, that have sent me down a Wonderland's rabbit hole to understand the different ways people think, feel and behave within the environment created, in response to their life experiences. It's an investigation through a cycle of curiosity, exploration, wondering and knowing. Along my journey, I can sense the signalling of the feel-good dopamine reward every time I've empirically proved what I've read in my Neuroscience studies to understand how the brain shapes our experiences; I hope the Neuroscience community will forgive my simplistic way of relating to such studies in this book.

I regularly save snapshots on my electronic files with inspirational ideas I come across anywhere, using a mixture of sketches and photos that I capture, which may include nature, architecture, branding, inspiring quotations from books, product design and technology.

Travelling is still my main source of inspiration. When I travel for family holidays, I try to fit in visits to local historic or contemporary landmarks, usually ending up not being very popular if I overstay my contemplation of building details or objects that capture my attention away from family time. Similarly, when I travel for work to different regions of England, I love to discover what is unique about the area to influence the proposed design.

I assimilate my curiosity to acquire new design information to that of walking in the shoes of a person who is about to enter a healthcare building for the first time. I believe that curiosity is a desirable building feature, as an appealing external appearance is reassuring and has the power to create positive anticipation in people. As a result, feel-good dopamine starts to release signals that good things are about to happen, motivating exploration. Thereafter, further dopamine is released if a person's positive impression of the building's external appearance is complemented with an equally positive and memorable indoor experience. The feel-good burst of dopamine facilitates a person's rewiring of the brain with an intentionality to heal. Such an experience would be even more rewarding if preceded by knowledge of positive results and stories associated to the building.

The opposite is equally true. If a healthcare building doesn't communicate a feel-good first impression and instead creates an unnerving one, people's anxiety levels may increase as they face an unknown. Resultingly, their self-protection instincts will take over and they may choose to avoid entering the building, to the detriment of the healing process.

My approach to our projects' development is to spend time in genuinely understanding interpersonal relationships, becoming sensitive to other people's needs and listening to the voices of all stakeholders. I see my role as an enabler and driver of innovative ideas which arise from collective intelligence and discussions, to understand which ones are most appropriate for the building-users we design for. My aim is to create an adaptive environment, rather than trying to enforce my own vision.

I love to embrace our design team's creativity, including the projects' stakeholders and the valuable lessons derived from the diversity of backgrounds. Developing the brief, by exploring several ideas through design options, is probably the most democratic activity in the process, when I enjoy the blend, challenge and development of new ideas. During the convergent thinking of the following stages of the design development, the shortlisted design options are subject to a fearless and continuous process of review and refining, to achieve incremental improvements, working collaboratively with the client and design team to craft special places. This becomes an intriguing discovery process, accompanied by a mixture of emotions, to understand what has value and how it can be amplified to inspire people and make them feel better both emotionally and physically.

Although there's no substitute for experiencing reality with our own senses, the use of 3D technology along with visualisations and above all virtual reality, has transformed our creative industry. It's proving particularly helpful to understand how the end-user emotionally responds to a virtual mock-up of an environment, for instance, how the texture or light reflectance values of a particular flooring design can help or hinder the viewer's perception. This technology has enhanced our design process, allowing us to collaboratively develop the art of the possible behind our ideas to positively engage, challenge, encourage and enthuse our clients.

As previously mentioned, it's not only essential for me to identify people's needs, but also to understand how to connect to the location or setting in which our designs will be used. Without a physical context, a design challenge on paper, risks becoming a pure vision, which can't ascertain people's feedback as to whether or not the project will deliver for the end-users.

Creative Wellbeing

Through the lens of my own experience, I like to understand the circumstances or factors which affect the way in which people live or work; how to harness the collective and creative energy to achieve wellbeing and how to create a synergistic environment. Each project journey is a celebration of the project team and its culture, it's a new opportunity to craft a space that defines people's new experiences.

The experience behind every project is a story that reveals something deeper about the people involved in the project, with passion and curiosity we explore a design that aims to engage and elicit an emotional response from the building-user. The story uses empathy to see the world from someone else's perspective, to understand what people see, how they see it and which options our design offers to unveil what we've seen. It's a memorable journey to discover the opportunities of a project to make people feel intuitively at ease with the surrounding environment, without the conditioning of an ego.

At the heart of this process is the design of a place with a personality that aims to engage all the senses, to be relatable with empathy, to help influence the human experience with positive energy and inclusive psychological support: using a combination of colours, materiality and quality of space, we can give people a sense of hope and optimism.

I've come to believe that to support people's wellbeing, the essence of my creativity is to be able to tolerate insecurity and resolve any ambiguity. Throughout my journey, I've worked on developing an awareness of myself and others, while remaining sensitive, passionate and committed; for me these are the important factors of being an architect, which are inextricably linked to nurturing a deeper empathic bond with the planet. It's a way of adding layers of meaning that create a stronger symbiotic connection between the building-users and nature's life force.

Design & Meditation

I remember one year, during one of my childhood summer months spent at our country house (campagna), in the absence of today's distractions from television and video games, I used to spend time under the shade of a Carob tree reading a book about a collection of fairy tales written by Hans Christian Andersen (a Danish author). The following extract made an impression on me, as it defines the essence of nature in our lives: "Just living isn't enough", said the butterfly, "one must have sunshine, freedom and a little flower".

This isn't a new concept; our ancestors intuitively understood the importance of the relationship between human nature and the natural environment, without any published research about how contact with nature benefits people. In history many Masters have integrated inspiration from nature's forms and processes in their work. For example, the garden courtyards of the Alhambra in Spain are a classic example of nature integrated in the built environment. Other examples are Leonardo da Vinci's studies to create a precursor of a flying machine and Art Nouveau's organic forms and lines. In the words of Rudolf Steiner, an Austrian polyhedric cultural figure and architect of the 19th century, "…knowledge of nature becomes a real wisdom".

In recent years I've closely followed how contemporary design contributes to the development of scientific research on biophilic design. When you think about it, there's no originality that nature, in truth, hasn't already explored to find the best way to make the most of the surrounding environment. Observing nature as a guide and trying to understand how it has adapted to the functions and contexts that are relevant to our projects, inspires my imaginative expressions. Nature is a book, full of wonders and inspiration, that we can read from every day, to learn how to live in balance with it; using our sensitivity to understand that we are part of something amazing that can help us with fresh ideas. We should aim to regain our ancestors' humility and reverence to work with nature.

In my studies I've learnt that nature's soundscape with its rich high and low frequencies can have a purifying, healing and nourishing effect on people; another demonstration that human beings and nature are a team, wherein each contributes to an interdependent whole. It's a relationship that I've embraced with our projects' empirical research with the question: what can we do to support the relationship between human beings and nature?

In direct contrast with my hospital stay, the buildings we design aim to promote wellbeing by exploring ways to develop a closer relationship with nature: creating comfortable indoor spaces with inspiring artwork; attractive colour schemes; sound-absorbing ceilings and flooring; soothing background music and appealing materials that are easy to clean. Accessing research on Biophilic design has offered further evidence on the healing effect of nature and how best to integrate it to support people's wellbeing with: engaging views of landscaped gardens and access to outdoor spaces; natural light and circadian artificial lighting and improved air quality and ventilation.

Recently the remodelling and refurbishment of Humber Teaching NHS Foundation Trust's office headquarters gave us the opportunity to explore what we've learnt about the benefits of biophilia associated to wellbeing in a healing environment and transfer it to an office, where it's important to reduce stress, enhance creativity and clarity of thought. The brief for the refurbishment was simple: to improve functionality with a combination of spaces that include both open plan offices and collaborative areas. However, we were determined to do more than just that, we wanted to explore the relationships between nature, people and the designed environment; an environment that supports the type of work being done by the fantastic people working for the Trust. We achieved this by creating simple layouts which promote efficient circulation and aesthetically-appealing interiors that holistically support health and wellbeing. If we dedicate time and resources to support those who support us, imagine how much more of a positive impact we could create together.

For the development of our biophilic design strategy, we adopted the three categories identified by the research paper "14 Patterns of Biophilic Design" published by Terrapin Bright Green, LLC: Nature in the Space, Natural Analogues and Nature of the Space.

Nature in the Space - As you enter the office, a living wall behind the reception is a pleasant introduction for the staff and visitors' visual connection, with indoor potted plants and furniture integrating a bespoke and dedicated planting tray present in most rooms. Large, glazed screens are available all around the building, which facilitate a visual connection with the landscaped outdoor areas and its seasonal changes. They're furnished with blinds, which are essential to maximise and diffuse the use of natural light and openable windows, which allow natural cross-ventilation and users' control to adjust the environment's temperature and airflow. Where the outdoor views were less inspiring or not possible, we integrated wallpaper with nature-themed scenes associated to the locality.

Natural Analogues – The colour scheme was devised to guide people's use of the space, creating a pervasive, rich, sensory connection with nature, particularly where this wasn't directly visible. For instance, the circulation area's light green ceiling makes the impression of being under the canopy of large trees, while the blinds project geometric shadows on walls, floors and ceilings that resemble leaves filtering the sunlight. The central collaborative space hosts kitchenette facilities and informal seating under a light blue ceiling with white and circular sound-absorbing suspended panels, which with their overlaps, resemble the gathering of geometrical clouds under a blue sky. The extensive use of wood veneers for the furniture and flooring with patterns similar to the natural veins of stones, facilitate an indirect connection with natural environments.

Nature of the Space – We created a balance of quiet focus areas which support a sense of withdrawal from the main activity areas; dedicated collaboration zones away from the desk, with internal screens completed with manifestations that offer a glimpse into adjacent rooms and high-energy social spaces, with sound-absorbing materials and colour contrasts. As a result, we created an inclusive design strategy, which also helps those with subtle physical disabilities such as challenges with hearing and sight, providing an environment that also caters for neurodiversity.

The personality of the space illustrated with my description of this project are very effectively analysed in Terrapin Bright Green, LLC's paper linking the biophilic design categories with biological responses associated to stress reduction, cognitive performance and emotion, mood and preference. The combination of categories used have the power to increase the health benefits of the space and the research paper confirms: "empirical evidence shows that positive emotions and mental restoration and other benefits can occur in as little as 5 to 20 minutes of immersion in nature" (Brown, Barton & Gladwell, 2013; Barton & Pretty, 2010; Tsunetsugu & Miyazaki, 2005).

To improve the building-users' experience, we integrated our biophilic design strategy with design principles studied in the WELL Building Standards, associated to four of the seven categories we felt we could have a direct influence on through our design: air, light, comfort, and mind. The environmental comfort features we introduced were particularly aimed at stress mitigation strategies to support the health and function of the systems in our bodies (cardiovascular, digestive, endocrine, immune, integumentary, muscular system, nervous, reproductive, respiratory, skeletal and urinary).

We didn't aim to achieve WELL certification, rather we used the WELL Building Standard Features Matrix to understand how best to optimise the environment using selected features. We particularly focused on the following features: Air (Ventilation effectiveness, VOC reduction, Fundamental material safety, Operable windows, Cleanable environment); Light (Visual lighting design, Solar glare control, Colour quality, Surface design); Comfort (ADA Accessible design standards, Ergonomics: visual and physical, Exterior noise intrusion, Internally generated noise, Thermal comfort, Olfactory comfort, Reverberation time, Sound masking, Sound reduction surfaces, Sound barriers) and Mind (Integrative design, Post-occupancy surveys, Beauty and design, Biophilia, Adaptable spaces and Material transparency).

Most design principles that I've adopted on my journey are based on published best practice and evidence-based research. If you've found any of the concepts mentioned of interest, I'd recommend further reading on the topic for a more profound insight.

~ ~ ~

I see a design solution as a blend of time, metaphor and vibration, which is rooted on a site and its energy; such energy needs to be drawn out from the site in a similar process to what people do when they listen to complex soundscapes, applying "auditory object formation" and "auditory object selection", which are linked to our experiences of past auditory scene analysis and attention. Similarly, our design solutions aim to harness the site's energy with compassion, maintaining a very sharp awareness of the surroundings and a focus on the project's details. The building's form follows the function without the need for the latter to become too prescriptive; a degree of flexibility is still required for the longevity of buildings which are in continuous evolution.

The key for me is being sensitive and respectful of the context's past, listening to everyone that allows us to define the future with our projects, using our creativity to challenge and work with the brief we've been given.

In line with the principles of Biomimicry, I find inspiration in nature through the practice of bio-inspired design. Amongst one of our healthcare projects recently completed for Hull University Teaching Hospitals NHS Trust, the vision for the award-winning Allam Diabetes Centre was to become a centre of excellence for diabetes. Therefore, the proposed design concept was based on the human body's organs affected by this condition. It was my approach to manifest the building's significance.

Our challenge for this building was to accommodate a complex accommodation program (which evolved during the design stage) including: waiting and reception areas; clinical and specialist treatment rooms; offices and collaborative research and training spaces over three storeys. In addition, the external areas were completed with a landscaped first floor terrace and landscaped surrounding areas integrating parking. Understanding the variety of functions and strategy helped us to understand the focus of the care provided and find inspiration for the biological theme that informed the design challenge.

The Allam Diabetes Centre provides a thoroughly modern facility, with tangible improvements to the patient experience, meeting the strategic vision for a flagship Diabetes Centre, attracting international and UK clinical teams. It is co-located within the main hospital's campus site boundary, with ready accessibility to the existing hospital diagnostic facilities and retinal screening services. This strengthens interdependencies with supporting clinical services and provides rapid access to the emergency response team. A key feature of the building is public, staff and patient accessibility, as many may have reduced mobility due to their conditions. In addition, there are relaxing and engaging public spaces and dedicated research and development areas, to further the Trust's excellent work on the next generation of treatments and care-plans.

As part of the preparatory work completed to define the building's design strategy, our design team analysed the urban context to identify local landmarks along the main traffic artery into the city centre, which could act as a reference and anchoring point for the design language. During the period of exploration and questions to understand the biology associated to diabetes metabolic disorder that could be translated into design solutions, we used cross-disciplinary brainstorming sessions, the results of which were simplified into sketches and diagrams. From this process, we learnt more about the care pathways' functions and mechanisms, which constituted the main project stakeholders' objectives. Another critical influence for the design was the Egyptian heritage of the benefactor, the late Dr Assem Allam, which inspired the minimalist curved volumes that characterise the building, along with the marble finish and gold-coloured window frames and aluminium trims. Gold held spiritual significance in ancient Egypt and is regarded as "the skin of the Gods. The resulting architectural presence conveys an expression of cultural and civic values. I particularly remember the first meeting with Dr Allam when, as I was sketching what the main elevation of the building would look like, he gently asked me for my pen and added his thoughts. It was a remarkable example of collaborative design.

The glazed main entrance and atrium isn't only a feature to create a welcoming embrace for building-users, but also an important connection with the seasonal stimuli of nature, such as cloud movements visible through the vaulted, glazed roof, combined with moderated variations in light and temperature. The naturally-lit street promotes health and is part of the building's energy-efficient system as well as being a clearly-defined central reference point to access the therapeutic and clinical accommodation provided on the flanking towers, where patients can find privacy for their consultation. The two towers' regular rhythm of openings, corresponding to the rooms provided, maximise the building's light, views, and ventilation control.

The building integrates a standardised design approach to provide future structural flexibility and adaptability. With exception of the lift core, all internal metal frame partitions are completely independent from the façade and the rhythmic positioning of openings helps achieve a flexible layout. The steel structure is distributed within the walls at the edge of each tower. Technically it will be possible to rearrange the façade (should it be required in future) since the cladding and the window sizes are designed to a standard dimension.

Maximising natural light and controlling ventilation was a key feature of pandemic-proof design to provide critical health benefits and was a main influence behind the design of the regular openings and the central glazed atrium. Furthermore, the building facilitates a one-way system, dedicated routes for staff changing areas and a zoning system to control the spread of infection.

It was important to dedicate an alternative space for patients and staff to congregate in an openly-ventilated and safe area, hence the garden terrace provides alternative views of the surroundings. Equally, the glazed parapet of the Juliette balconies complete the façade openings and offer a safe way to increase ventilation and interact with the external environment. Finally, the building finishes are easy to clean and compliant with healthcare guidance.

Hospital patients often feel intimidated as they approach the premises, therefore our proposed curved design, together with the glazed main entrance and atrium creates a welcoming effect to embrace people. In addition, the human scale, ground floor reception reinforces the de-institutionalised feel of the building.

As previously mentioned, the anatomy of the major organs affected by diabetes inspired the building's biomorphic plan, which was achieved through a continuous loop of emulation and evaluation to find a design essence that combined site and functions' constraints with the concept; the building's natural curved lines are a concept abstraction and deliberately avoid strict adherence to the complexity of biological principles, which would be too complex to convey visually. The building's psychological aesthetic was defined through several evaluation meetings with multi-disciplinary stakeholders, which evolved from early sketches into visualisations. Along the process, we developed prototypes of the façade's radius and associated finishing materials, which culminated in the selection of porcelain cladding.

Glazed surfaces, partly-shaded by perforated film with uniquely designed patterns inspired by the molecular structures of insulin, intertwine with solid panels. The complexity of the molecular structure mirrors the complexity of diabetes and the support required to keep people healthy. Therefore, the unique film introduces biophilic elements, working with natural light and shadows. Equally, the garden terrace provides patients and staff with a biophilic environment to support the healing therapies carried out within the building. These are all features of subtle communication, like a harmonious dance, where every move counts. Each gesture, signal, and unspoken message carries meaning, and its careful choice and execution can make all the difference to create a beautiful and dynamic experience.

The design is based on the WELL Design Standards and BREEAM (Building Research Establishment Environmental Assessment Method) which are leading Science-based validation and certification systems to achieve a sustainable built environment. Working for several public institutions, it's always been important to me to optimise all of our designs with sustainable solutions. In addition, we calculate our organisation's carbon emissions annually and offset them with tree planting schemes in the UK and abroad. I believe that during our lifetime each one of us needs to plant as many trees as possible, safe in the knowledge that our children may be able to sit under their shade one day.

Since completion of the building, our involvement has continued via informal post-occupancy evaluations, which focus on building-users' qualitative and sensory perceptions, to understand staff, patient and visitor perspectives.

The feedback received has helped us to understand first impressions and how the building conveys the care provided along its social and civic presence. In summary, the general feedback expressed that the building is instantly recognisable and memorable as it conveys dignity and respect for its building-users; it also benefits the city as a whole by enhancing the street scene and being recognised as a local landmark, which has won several healthcare design awards. The main staircase, visible through the glass from the outside, is one of the building's

recognisable features, motivating active movement and lifestyle, a strategy to prevent the likelihood of contracting diabetes. Overall, staff have confirmed pride of being part of a building that conveys the fantastic work of the NHS.

The details of a new project always fascinate me; if the project's design concept is a way of expressing my imagination, I need to ensure the accuracy of the design details is congruent with the concept's message, for the building to stand the test of time.

I had a further opportunity to design Porritt Care Home, a new build, bio-inspired care home, forming part of a care village development including an existing care home, on behalf of a Millennium Care. As I walked with the owner through the site's woodlands to establish the best location for the home, the healing power that such a multi-sensory setting must have on the existing care home's residents and surrounding community immediately struck me. The resulting design challenge emerged as to how I could ensure that the new man-made building would become an extension of the surrounding natural environment. I was inspired by the semi-rural, natural setting and specifically, the details associated to the vernacular drystone walling, which formed landscaped terraces offering calming views over the rolling hills of the English countryside.

My studies of people's visual preferences and responses to nature, reveals the incredible impact it has on our wellbeing. Visually connecting with nature reduces stress, improves concentration and enhances recovery rates.

The benefits go beyond physiological aspects such as lowering blood pressure, reducing concentration fatigue and decreasing negative emotions such as sadness, anger and aggression. Engaging with nature, whether in person or through images, boosts mental engagement, attentiveness, and overall happiness.

The vision for the care village developed with the client included: a new purpose-built, four-storey building, including a small number of en-suite bedrooms in clusters with ancillary accommodation on each floor; extra care apartments with associated communal facilities and external landscaped areas with parking. Furthermore, the vision was based upon studies of working practices in mainland Europe and specifically, in the Netherlands and Holland. Of particular significance is the dementia village and principles of the Buurtzorg Model in the Netherlands and the household model of care. This model focuses on providing home comforts and maintaining ties of kinship.

Principally, the idea is to create a small household setting, with an open plan kitchen/diner and lounge as the heart of activities, which promotes socialisation amongst the residents, staff and visitors.

The tranquil site, secluded by woodlands, lies just outside the market town of Ramsbottom in the north of England, with public pathways and beautiful views of the surrounding valley, for the wider community to enjoy. As previously mentioned, an existing care home currently operates on the site, from the adapted premises of an existing 1850's Mansion House, with some recent extensions. The existing buildings have millstone grit elevations and are generally two-storeys high, with duo pitched slate tiled roofs. The natural terrain has areas with a 45% gradient and the vernacular dry-stone walls support the existing system of terraces, which captured my attention, inspiring the location for the building. As a result, our design offers a simple volume, used as a retaining wall for a new terrace. The façade treatment is similar to the dry-stone walling, which enhances visual interest and a sense of cultural continuity. The building is oriented to maximise daylight and views of the surrounding woodland settings and the valley.

Our design captures the opportunities, interactions and relationships of its semi-rural, distinctive context, identified during the site analysis, which has resulted in an unobtrusive volume mediating the relationship between its users and nature. The building provides a delicate negotiation between the access to the landscape and its care and conservation balancing materials, size, and shapes. It's intended as an extension of the surrounding nature, acting as a subservient transition between the historic original building and the natural environment.

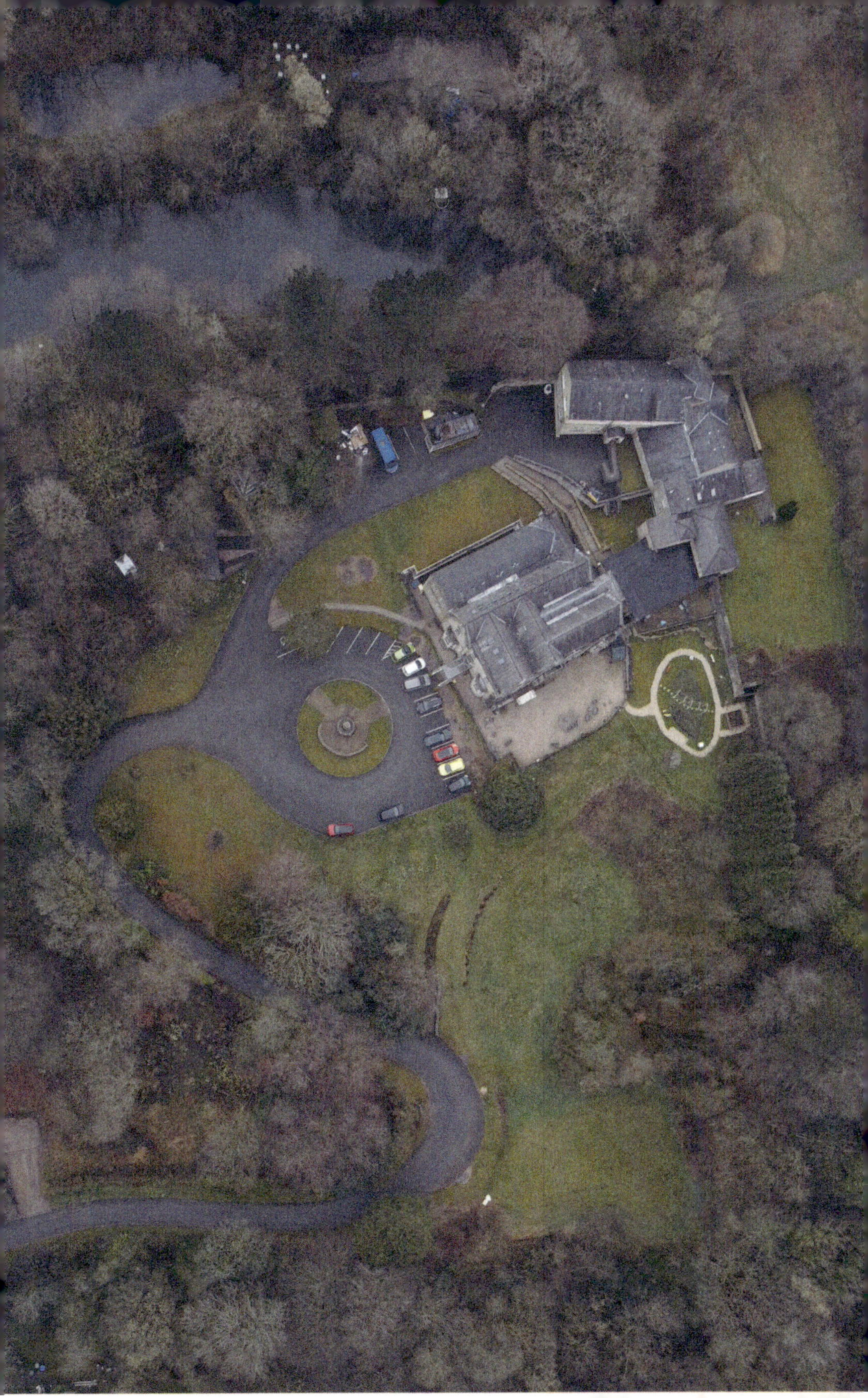

The proposed materials for the elevations' treatment, inspired by the rich and authentic woodland settings addresses many of the senses by way of its integration in the surrounding landscape. Natural materials used (natural stone in a random arrangement) allow a full integration with the surrounding random dry-stone masonry used to form terraces in the terrain. The stone walling of the façade terminates with raised flower beds, integrated within the parapet walls of the roof terrace, which offer several activities for the residents to interact with the natural setting; this will include bird watch refuge huts as well as opportunities to engage many of the senses: visual, haptic, olfactory, gustatory and auditory.

The building's layout has been refined throughout an iterative process, which included several design developments and evaluation meetings with prospective users, families, project and community stakeholders. Above all, the aim is to support residents' empowerment, enabling them to retain control for as long as possible. By creating a simple plan form, the design generates a logical layout that makes navigation easier for residents. A simple palette of surface materials has also been used to establish a visual connection with the proposed building and to aid orientation. It's vital to design environments that provide individuals with the option to make positive use of the space outside of their private quarters. To achieve this, we've developed a variety of rooms with different characters, offering endless opportunities for socialisation or contemplation, supported by the visual and physical full immersion in natural settings.

Within the surrounding landscape, the scheme aims to create attractive communal gardens and terraces for the residents' wellbeing; providing attractive views from the building throughout the year, opportunities for gardening, access to fresh air and simple relaxation. We introduced richly-planted, raised flower beds which provide a fully-accessible, outdoor amenity for residents, visitors and staff, which offers sensory qualities while enhancing and contributing to the local biodiversity. The planting provides multi-sensory stimulation with seasonal colours, textures, scents, and movement to encourage the residents' physiological restoration.

The main entrance is close to the existing building and is clearly visible on approach. Furthermore, a dedicated set of steps and ramps overcome the differences in levels and an adjacent drop-off point assists residents to access the buildings. In addition, the entrance is clearly marked by a glazed curtain wall and a canopy. The proposed, brightly-lit, spacious foyer inside the entrance provides a vibrant heart to the scheme and creates an informal meeting area with plenty of space for seating and socialising. Finally, the surrounding landscaped gardens and courtyards provide an extension to the communal areas with large, glazed openings, which offer delightful views; it's widely recognised that having an abundance of daylight within a building encourages the improvement of residents' health and well-being.

The main entrance's central location facilitates access to the main communal areas which are the social heart of each floor. From these areas, a progressive privacy strategy caters for the residential areas of the building; corridors end with arrival points featuring ample natural light and enjoyable views over the gardens. The building not only offers a unique experience for each resident, but also respects the plot's topography with a sequence of steps, rotations and intermediate terraces, that provide framed views over the valley, plenty of natural light and ventilation.

Your turn...
What is the harmonious frequency of your language?

Foreground

"The power of the world always works in circles,
and everything tries to be round.
The sky is round, and I have heard
that the earth is like a ball,
and so are the stars.
The wind, in its greatest power, whirls;
Birds make their nests in circles,
For theirs is the same religion as ours.
The sun and moon, both round,
Come forth and go down again in circle.
Even the seasons form a great circle in their changing,
And always come back again to where they were.
The life of a person is a circle from childhood to childhood,
And so it is in everything where power moves."

- Black Elk

The word empathy is derived from the Ancient Greek empatheia, meaning "physical affection or passion". The word derives from ἐν ("in, at") and πάθος, "passion", associated to the word "design" it signifies for me "putting feeling into design".

As you will have gathered from what you have read so far, this book was not conceived to provide solutions, it's rather the introspective exploration of a learning strategy which adopts critical questions to understand personal emotions in relation to an existential context and how an empathic design can help people to transform any negative emotions into positive ones. In the process I find it important to identify what is the emotional state people experience in their environment using questions that allow us to delve deeper into the understanding of how the environment makes people feel. Visualisation is a powerful tool to train our brains; when you imagine an action, the same brain patterns are activated as when you physically perform it. This is why the use of immersive 3D visualisations has been at the heart of our design process from the outset, to help us gain valuable feedback to design a positive environment that supports people, enhancing the outcome.

I believe that a design focused on wellbeing can drive social and cultural transformation, going beyond what people can afford. Architecture at its best is a meditative journey to learn profound lessons through intuitive thoughts, service, craft, personalisation, and style which requires discipline, focus and depth of experience. It doesn't need an end, because every project is an investigation into the essence of making it a perfect fit for each individual and as such, forever different; it has the power to communicate with people in subtle ways, with a focus on possibility rather than the opposite, to inspire change and to bring people together. The grounding words of Maya Angelou, an American poet, have become an important reference in my journey: "Do the best you can until you know better.

Then when you know better, do better." Studying design, health and wellbeing to date has opened up several other areas of interest for me, with surprise findings which have reaffirmed my commitment to delve deeper to into my studies over the coming years. At this stage, my studies into Architecture, Art, Neuroscience, Psychology, Philosophy, Sociology and culture connected to my own context, have been critical to refine my designs to date.

According to the philosopher Immanuel Kant, reality is only based on individual perception, which is routed in our belief system. Our designs aim to reach out to people to illustrate what a different perception can offer, holding a mirror from our experiences. It's an organic design process that aims to bridge the gap between different sections of a community, providing a holistic experience that goes beyond the first impression of the fabric of the building; the relationship is carried forward with the visual, tactile and acoustic comfort conveyed by the interior design scheme, to create the perfect setting to enjoy any of the activities performed in a building that has its own personality and conveys a sense of purpose.

The space where we spend most of our time can have an immense impact on our mental state, productivity and overall health. An empathic design can provide environments that exude positivity, energise every individual and impart a sense of acceptance. By providing diverse spaces, supporting psychological needs and embracing the uniqueness of everyone, empathetic design can significantly enhance our wellbeing. The projects illustrated have design elements in common of a space that is inclusive and sustainable, relatable to people and supportive of their emotions.

A well-designed environment has the power to influence our approach to life and relationships with a calm, non-reactive, and optimistic attitude. Wellness is more than just proper nutrition and exercise – it encompasses the total energy environment in which we live. At the heart of my design philosophy is a commitment to an empathic design, which I believe is especially relevant to the health sector, but certainly not limited to it.

Ultimately, the real difference-maker has been working with clients who share our passion for engaging with all stakeholders and pushing the boundaries of what's possible. By investing their time and providing additional motivation, they've enabled us to create designs that make a positive impact and withstand the rigours of value engineering sessions. In the end, what gives us the greatest satisfaction is knowing that the design created helps people feel valued and supported.

Teamwork is what makes our relationships, characterised by openness and empathy, respect and participation, defined by our actions rather than by our appearances and beliefs. I enjoy sharing meaningful successes and the rewards of what we've achieved through our projects with the people we work with and for. We design together using empathy to increase our ability to see, hear and feel; to discover the human experiences that differ from our own; through giving and receiving inspiration, we unlock our potential both personally and professionally, hopefully the projects completed will help others become aware of their emotions to unlock their potential.

In the words of Jules Renard, a French author: *"If I were to begin life again, I should want it just as it was; only I would open my eyes a little more."*

Afterword
by Amelia Caruso

After almost 25 years together, Alessandro and I usually know what to expect from one another, but on a few occasions, he has really taken me by surprise. For example, although we'd always mentioned how nice it would be to work together, I never actually thought we'd set up Alessandro Caruso Architecture & Interiors Ltd (ACA), which we are still running together ten years on. Similarly, I didn't foresee myself writing an Afterword for this book, as I couldn't imagine Alessandro having the time nor the energy to write it and dedicate himself to anything other than his passion; designing buildings to improve peoples' lives. Even my mother-in-law was surprised by this book, as she told me it was a struggle to get Alessandro to read as a child! There's nothing like being kept on your toes!

Alessandro and I are complete opposites in many ways, which is what attracted us to each other in the beginning. According to astrology, our zodiac signs are polar opposites too, although the combination is usually complementary, as each sign compensates for the qualities the other lacks. This is what we have found in our marriage, as parents and running the business together. Having said that, we do share some similarities. Like Alessandro, when I was younger, I also had a yearning to travel and believe that our separate quests to discover what was beyond our immediate horizons eventually led us to each other. Against all odds and people saying that our relationship would fail rather than flourish, we have followed our hearts and been guided to pursue opportunities where we can excel together.

When we first made the leap of faith to be together and I moved to Sicily, we thought that was where we would stay as Alessandro was establishing himself in the family business. We had no idea that only a year later, we would be exploring work options back in the UK. For this reason, I'm immensely proud of Alessandro for leaving his home country and facing various challenges to accomplish what he has achieved in my country. Nothing has come easy and just as our will to be together was tested to the maximum, there have been several obstacles to overcome before being able to start fulfilling his mission. Alessandro has not only developed a successful career in a foreign country but has also distilled an essential alphabet for a harmonious language to communicate "empathic design", which he explores in this book.

From my perspective, this book contains certain ingredients selected along Alessandro's journey, to conceive his designs for buildings which improve peoples' lives. A Buddhist Zen Monk told Alessandro that the duty of the Zen Chef is to prepare the best meal with the ingredients available, even if only water and rice. I recognise Alessandro's core ingredients as six Ps: Purpose, Passion, Patience, Practice, Partnerships and Perception.

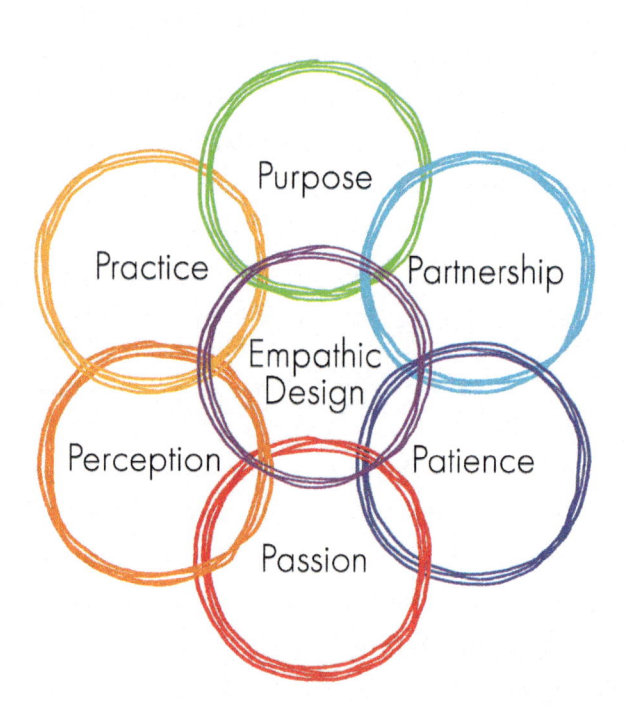

Purpose: Alessandro's accident forced him to stop and with not much else to do, to take a good look at his life and learn an important lesson. From this unfortunate event, a calling, or true purpose arose. As both an architecture student and patient confined to a hospital bed, Alessandro developed a dual perspective of how a person-centred building needed to be designed, to have a positive impact on the people in it. A catalogue of bad design factors and the negative effects of them on his own mental health and wellbeing boldly highlighted exactly what was required to do the opposite for the design of his future buildings. This purpose forms the basis of ACA's mission which is to design buildings which improve peoples' quality of lives.

Passion: Upon eventual recovery and grateful for a second chance at life, a passion was ignited inside Alessandro to fulfil his new purpose. Once he realised the extent to which the design of a building can either positively or negatively impact the people in it, he hasn't stopped learning and refining how to design well, in any context. A one-size-fits-all recipe doesn't exist, as each project begins with a blank slate, with completely different building-users and requirements. There may be some common elements, but what are the proportions? As Marc Anthony said: "If you do what you love, you'll never work a day in your life" which rings true for Alessandro. He goes beyond the role of an architect, in his continuous quest for research, improvement and the sharing of best practice.

Patience: Rome wasn't built in a day. Alessandro has had to learn to be patient on many occasions. The long and arduous recovery and rehabilitation process of the accident was one occasion. Moving to the UK as a qualified Italian architect and accepting an initial backward career step was another. Waiting out the first year of setting up ACA when there were no clients nor fees in sight was another. Being married to me is another! As the saying goes, patience is a virtue and has made Alessandro resilient and tenacious when the going gets tough.

Practice: Turning to spirituality and the discipline of meditation is a coping mechanism for stress and pain, which has become a real game-changer for Alessandro. Not only does it allow also him to briefly quieten his overactive mind, but in these moments, he often finds clarity, when the answers come to him. It is a valuable practice which allows him to reflect and strengthen his faith, which helps in times when patience is required.

Partnerships: Alessandro couldn't deliver the projects he designs on his own. It is important to find people with similar values to be able to bring a building to life from concept to reality. ACA's apprentices are hungry to learn, believe in ACA's mission and are empowered to excel in their areas of strength. Through healthy and long-term consultants' and suppliers' partnerships, lessons learnt can be carried out and built upon on the next project, rather than starting from scratch. The majority of ACA's clients provide repeat business as they value the importance placed on partnerships and people.

Perception: Emotional intelligence, or an awareness of self and others is key. Alessandro's understandings of his own emotions in response to the hospital environment he experienced at the time of his accident, became a reflection of what others may feel in different environments. With this knowledge, at the start of every project, Alessandro ensures that he asks as many questions as possible to all stakeholders, to accurately capture the brief. Without active listening and consolidating requirements, how can he design a people-centred building?

Something that stood out to me when working on this book, is that Alessandro innately captures all levels of Maslow's hierarchy of needs in his designs, without trying. Any architect will design to address physiological, safety and security needs as a minimum. Where I see Alessandro adding value is by incorporating the rest as staple. He considers social needs such as the need for interpersonal relationships and a sense of belonging by creating communal spaces which encourage social connections. This is evident particularly in care home and extra care designs such as household care models with focal points such as a warm fireplace, a piano or landscaped outdoor spaces. Similarly, office and education designs include vibrant and motivational social spaces.

Esteem needs are considered by offering a building-user choices based on the creation of an immersive and inclusive experience. Another way is the creation of spaces that reflect individual and cultural identity. Working with local artists to incorporate the spirit of the locality enhances the interior design schemes, instilling local cultural sensitivities into a building. Architectural expression through immersive design, where form follows function stimulating the senses, contributes to a sense of dignity and pride for building-users. Iconic, award-winning buildings such as the Allam Diabetes Centre and the Community Diagnostic Centre also instil a collective sense of esteem within the community.

Self-Actualisation needs are addressed by designing spaces that inspire creativity, personal growth and a sense of purpose. ACA's office and college designs facilitate self-actualisation by offering environments that encourage learning, exploration and the pursuit of individual passions.

There have been a few challenges in writing this book. I think we both underestimated the input required and finding the time to dedicate to working on the book on top of running the Practice. Furthermore, Alessandro has never been a man of many words, but of very complex and philosophical thoughts. His brain just never stops and his vocabulary can barely keep up, so he tends to stay quiet, reflecting and is often in his own world.

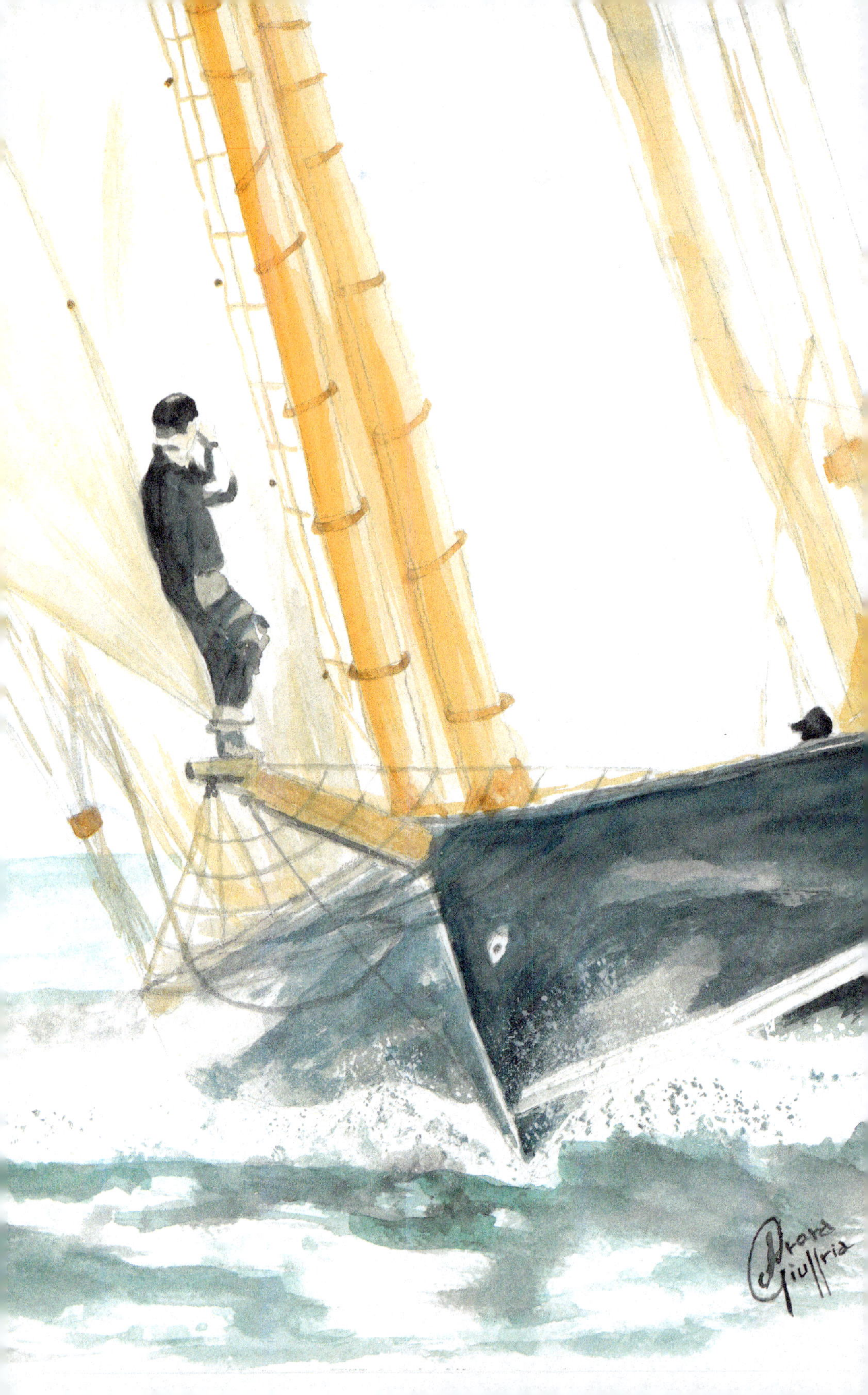

Acknowledgements

I mentioned earlier in the book how my accident became a catalyst for the awakening of empathic skills I'd not cared to develop until then. It is equally true that I wouldn't have been able to practice my awareness of these important skills without the help of my wife Amelia who, as a partner in life and in business, has patiently and consistently believed in me, topping up my oxytocin levels when I needed it! Your contribution to anything that I have done in our life together has always been substantial. As you know well, for me writing does not come easy and this book could not have happened without your help and support in finding expressions that are clear and accessible to all, simplifying where necessary my whirling expressions in a language that is not mine. The unconventional and unflinching way we met and have stuck together with our complementarity of views has been a value which continues to influence our personal and professional lives together.

The next special thanks belong to our daughters, Roberta and Gabriella, who have accompanied us in our journey so far, lovingly putting up with the pressures that a family business demands, while trying to understand some of the issues that inevitably infiltrated conversations at the dinner table or family time. I hope the curiosity of our travelling time together, seeing puzzling places of interest for me, rubs off on you to find your passion in life and use your creative skills to develop your own voice and fulfilling collaborations.

Like many of our projects, this book has not been individually produced and I am grateful to all that have contributed in one way or another to every moment of my journey. Particular thanks to the team who I am fortunate to have around to support me patiently over the last few years as well as inspire me with their skills and wits; to the clients and colleagues from complementary disciplines outside our organisation with whom every collaboration offers a new experience to learn from and motivate us to achieve more.

I wish to express a special appreciation to Dr Wayne Ruga for helping me to unlock the important themes in my life and work over the last few years which has enabled the writing of this book. Your attentive listening and motivational thoughts have been a critical factor in pushing me outside of my comfort zone to write my first book.

To David Nurse for the opportunity he gave me when I first arrived in the UK. I remain in awe of his patience and wit to always make me think about the choices I was about to make, in my transformative journey towards becoming a more humble self, helping me to see the importance hope plays in the design process.

To all the people that I have been lucky enough to meet in my journey and have contributed to my career development either directly or indirectly, challenging any ideas explored together.

To all my friends who genuinely support me with joyful memories and inspire me with ever engaging conversations.

I am also grateful to who fuelled my determination for a greater personal spiritual growth away from my native Sicily, I may have not achieved it without a challenge.

To my English family for showing me the quirkiness of English life and putting up with my ever-demanding schedules.

To my brother and sister, Enrico and Marcella, and their extended families for sharing part of the journey, supporting me despite our geographical distances.

Finally and by no means lastly, to my parents, Iole and Franco, who have helped me and supported me in more than one way along the journey and for leaving the blank wall of that play room at the heart of our family home, which allowed my creative pursuits to get started.

Recommended readings

Books

R. Buckminster Fuller: *Critical Path. St Martin's Griffins*, 1981
Italo Calvino: *Mr Palomar*. Vintage Classics, 1994
Richard P. Feinman: *Il senso delle cose,* Adelphi, 1999
Europan, Concursos Europeos para Arquitectura. 10 años Europan 5 España, ZAC Diseno Grafico, 1999
His Holiness Dalai Lama: *The Dalai Lama's Little Book of Wisdom,* Harper Collins Publishers, 2002
Damien Keown: *Buddhist Ethics,* Oxford, 2005
Nyogen Senzaki, Paul Reps: *101 Storie Zen,* Adelphi, 2000
George Leonard: *Mastery. A Plume Book,* 1992
Ronald A. Heifetz: *Leadership without Easy Answers,* Belknap Harvard, 1994
George Leonard: *The Silent Pulse,* E.P. Dutton, 1978
Richard Gerber: *A Practical Guide to Vibrational Medicine,* Harper, 2001
Jacob Liberman: *Light: Medicine of the Future,* Bear & Company, 1991
Manfred Clynes: *Sentics: The Touch of Emotions,* Knopf Doubleday Publishing Group, 1977
David Robson: *The Intelligence Trap,* Hodder. 2020
John Hegarty: *Hegarty on Creativity,* Thames & Hudson, 2014
Juhani Pallasmaa: *The Eyes of The Skin: Architecture and the Senses,* Wiley. 2013
Mario Botta, Paolo Crepet: *Dove Abitano le Emozioni,* Einaudi, 2007
Edward T. Hall: *The Silent Language,* Anchor books, 1990
Edward T. Hall: *The Hidden Dimension*, Anchor Books, 1982

Erving Goffman, *The Presentation of Self in Everyday Life*, Penguin Books, 1959
Erving Goffman: *Stigma: Notes on the Management of Spoiled Identity*, Penguin Books, 1963
John Waitzkin: *The Art of Learning*, Free Press, 2007
Frank Lloyd Wright: *An Autobiography*, Horizon Press, 1997
Michael Pawlin: *Biomimicry in Architecture*, RIBA Publishing, 2016
Sophia and Stefan Behlin: *Sol Power: The Evolution of Solar Architecture*, Prestel, 1996
Christian Schittich: *In Detail: Solar Architeture*, Birkhauser, 2003
Christopher Alexander, *A Pattern Language*, Oxford University Press, 1977
Steen Eiler Rasmussen: *Experiencing Architecture*, The MIT Press, 1959
Alain De Botton: *Architecture of Happiness*, Penguin Books, 2006
Christopher Day: *Places of the Soul*, Architectural Press, 2004
Pablo Palazuelo: *Geometria y Vision*. Diputacion Provincial de Granada, 1995

Journals

Evidence Based Design Journal

Articles

William Browning, Catherine Ryan, Joseph Clancy: *14 patterns of biophilic design*, Terrapin Bright Green, 2014
Mark Hammond, Nigel Saunders: *A Design for Life:* Manchester Metropolitan University Press, 2021
Dana Dubbs: *Unlocking The Brain For Better Architecture And Design*, 2005
Mardelle M. Shepley, Samira Pasha: *Design Research And Behavioral Health Facilities*, 2013
Richard Fleming, John Zeisel, Kirsty Bennett: *World Alzheimer Report*, 2020

Websites

Home - Alessandro Caruso Architects *aca-i.com*
Design In Mental Health *dimhn.org*
Dementia Services Development Centre *stir.ac.uk*
Academy *designhealth.academy*
Architects for Health – *architectsforhealth.com*
ANFA | Homepage *anfarch.org*
WELL v1 Standard | IWBI *wellcertified.com*
What is BREEAM? - BRE Group *bregroup.com/products/breeam*
Authentic Yoga for Your Well-being | Akhanda Yoga Institute – Akhanda Yoga Wellbeing & AY Institute *akhandayoga.com*
Home | Erasmus+ *europa.eu*
2030 Climate Challenge *architecture.com/about/policy/climate-action/2030-climate-challenge*

Audiobooks/Podcast

Rudolf Steiner: *Audio*, Audible
Nikola Tesla: *My Inventions*, Blackstone Audio, 2017
Helen Shuman: *A course in Miracles,* 2018

About the author

Alex is an architect and co-founder of Alessandro Caruso Architecture and Interiors Ltd, an award winning Practice based in Beverley, United Kingdom.

Being fluent in three languages and having gained over 25 years of professional experience in design across England, Spain and his native Italy, Alex understands the importance of establishing clear communication from the earliest sketches. Adopting three-dimensional technologies to translate client requirements into a design accessible to a much wider audience, his mission is to improve people's wellbeing through sustainable design.

Alex views design as a "lifelong learning" journey, constantly presenting new opportunities for form to follow function while engaging the senses. He draws inspiration from his studies and his extensive global network of contacts.

Alex is a RIBA Client Advisor who firmly believes in sharing knowledge and best practices to support clinical delivery. He frequently delivers speeches and presents lessons derived from his completed projects at conferences, conventions, colleges and universities.

He lives in the United Kingdom, where he conducts most of his design studies and observations, capturing them in writings and conference talks.

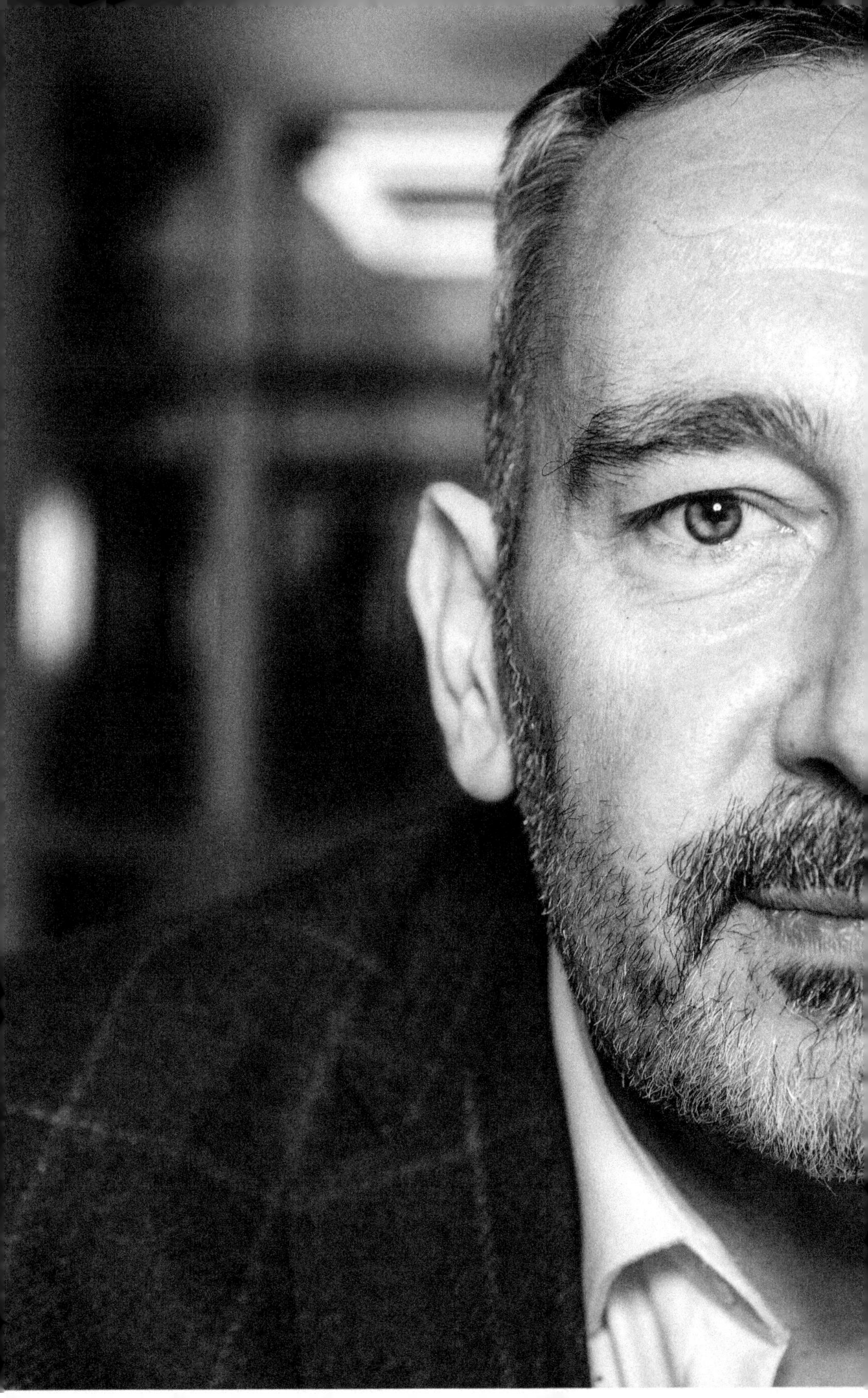

Photo credits

Abbeyfield/Linda Schwab/Alessandro Caruso Architects: 137, 138, 140
Alessandro Caruso Architects: 25, 48, 95, 114, 116, 180, 191
Assenza Massimo: front cover, 13, 72, 105
Caruso Alessandro: 24, 32, 43, 44, 74, 110
Caruso Amelia: 178, 183
Caruso Francesco: 35, 36, 37, 38, 153
Edgar Alice: 71, 99,
Francis Leo: 57, 193
Finch Andrea: 64/65, 66/67
Giuffria Aurora: 21, 184
Hull Teaching Hospitals NHS Trust/Insight Photography: 125, 159, 160, 161, 165
Humber Teaching NHS Foundation Trust/Alessandro Caruso Architects: 102/103, 119, 131, 132, 155, 156
Millenium Care Group/Alessandro Caruso Architects: 166, 169, 170, 172
Олег Арзамасцев: 55
Pickpick.com: 91
Priory Group: 144, 145, 146, 147
Public domain: 40, 77, 85, 124, 135
St Barnabas Hospice/Stefano Cavallini: 115, 121, 129

The Ran Network
https://therannetwork.com

Printed in Great Britain
by Amazon